ENDANGERED!

HAWKS & FALCONS

John Woodward

Series Consultant: James G. Doherty
General Curator, The Bronx Zoo, New York

BENCHMARK BOOKS

MARSHALL CAVENDISH
NEW YORK

Benchmark Books
Marshall Cavendish Corporation
99 White Plains Road
Tarrytown, New York 10591-9001

Library of Congress Cataloging-in-Publication Data

Woodward, John, 1954-
     Hawks & Falcons / by John Woodward.
          p.   cm. — (Endangered!)
     Includes index.
     Summary: Describes the physical characteristics, habitat, and
behavior of different kinds of hawks and falcons and discusses how
to save these birds of prey from extinction.
     ISBN 0-7614-0293-4
     1. Hawks—Juvenile literature.   2. Falcons—Juvenile literature.
3. Endangered species—Juvenile literature. [1. Hawks.
2. Falcons. 3. Endangered species.] I. Title. II. Series.
QL696.F32W675 1997
598.9'16—dc20   96-7221
                                                                       CIP
                                                                       AC

Printed and bound in the United States

PICTURE CREDITS
The publishers would like to thank the Frank Lane Picture Agency for
supplying all the photographs used in this book except for the following: 8, BC
Ardea; 11, 27 Bruce Coleman Ltd; 5 Natural History Photographic Agency.

Series created by Brown Packaging

Front cover: Peregrine.
Title page: Osprey.
Back cover: Peregrine chasing pigeon.

Contents

Introduction

A giant tortoise makes a fine perch for this Galapagos hawk. The Galapagos hawk is found only on the Galapagos Islands in the Pacific, where there may be only 300 left.

Hawks and falcons are among the most exciting of all birds. Some are high-speed hunters that chase other birds through the air and kill them on the wing. Others search for small animals on the ground, soaring or hovering high above them before diving down for the kill.

Hawks are small to medium-sized **birds of prey**, with sharp, hooked bills for tearing flesh. They have fantastic eyesight for pinpointing **prey** from a distance and powerful **talons** for catching and killing their victims. Hawks can be

4

divided into a number of groups, including ospreys, forest hawks, harriers, and kites.

Falcons are also birds of prey, but are different enough from hawks for scientists to group them separately. For example, unlike hawks, falcons rarely build nests. Most lay their eggs on cliffs or ledges. Like hawks, though, they are known by many different names. Kestrels are falcons, as is the peregrine.

Hawks and falcons have **adapted** to living in all sorts of places and can survive all kinds of natural hardship. Even so, many are in danger of becoming **extinct** because of people's actions. In this book, we will enter the world of hawks and falcons to discover how they live and why they are in danger. Let's start by looking at some well-known falcons that are at risk – the peregrine and the kestrels.

A peregrine falcon swoops down on its prey. Fast and powerful, the peregrine can reach speeds of up to 125 miles per hour (200 km/h) in its hunting dive.

Falcons

The falcons are the most spectacular birds of prey. Most **species** hunt by chasing other birds through the open sky, so they are built for speed. They have long, pointed wings to push them through the air. Some falcons, on the other hand, have an ability to hover in one spot as they search for small animals on the ground. These small falcons are known as kestrels.

Unlike hawks, which kill with their feet, falcons sometimes kill with their bills. A falcon's bill is sharp and has a special notch like a pair of wire-cutters that gives it a good grip as it bites through the neck of its victim.

With its tail fanned out to act as a brake, a European kestrel reaches out to snatch its prey from the grass.

Peregrines

The most well-known falcon is the peregrine. A muscular bird with a steel-gray back and a pale breast barred with black, it has a dark head with black streaks beneath its black, yellow-rimmed eyes. The peregrine falcon is found almost everywhere in the world but varies in size depending on where it lives. The biggest live in the Far North: an Alaskan peregrine may grow up to 19 inches (48 cm) long. As is the case with most other birds of prey, the female is much bigger than the male.

The peregrine is famous for its amazing way of hunting. Instead of chasing birds through the air, it usually dives

A peregrine brings food to its young at the nest. This cliff nesting site may have been used by peregrines for hundreds of years.

from high in the sky to take them by surprise. The speed of the attack is awesome, and the midair collision is often enough to kill the prey right away.

Peregrines are particularly fond of eating pigeons, and this has gotten them into a lot of trouble. During World War II, most of the peregrines living on English coasts were shot to keep them from killing pigeons carrying important messages from France. Even today, peregrines are sometimes illegally shot by **gamekeepers** and people who race pigeons.

A few years after World War II, peregrines in northern countries began suffering from **pesticide** poisoning, mainly from eating birds that had eaten pesticide-soaked seeds.

If a peregrine misjudges its first attack, it can use its speed to overtake its prey as it tries to escape. In this instance its prey is a pigeon.

8

Many peregrines failed to produce young because one of the pesticide chemicals – DDT – made the shells of their eggs so thin that they broke in the nest. This led to the peregrine almost disappearing from Europe and North America in the 1950s and 1960s.

Once the cause of the problem was known, DDT and similar chemicals were made illegal in most northern countries, and the numbers of peregrines started to increase once again. In some **tropical** regions, however, DDT has not been banned. In Africa, for example, it is used to kill mosquitoes that carry diseases like malaria. Many kinds of tropical falcons are still in danger from pesticide poisoning.

Areas where the peregrine can be found

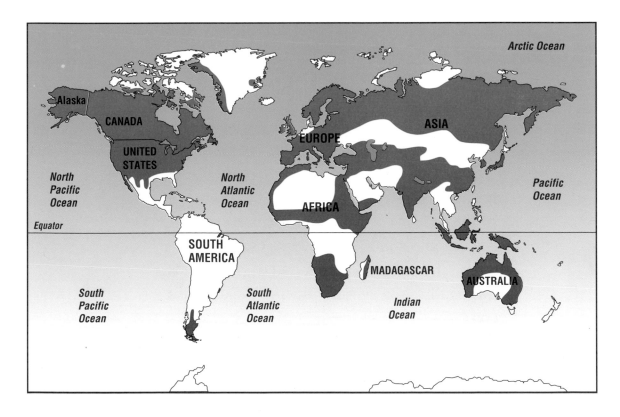

Areas where the lesser kestrel can be found

Kestrels

Not all kestrels are in danger, but some are suffering because people have changed the landscape. In southern Europe the lesser kestrel is becoming rare because its grassland **habitat** has been turned into farmland or built over. About 12 inches (30 cm) long, the lesser kestrel has a red-brown back. In females, the head is also red-brown, while that of the male is blue-gray. The bird hunts as most kestrels do, hovering over open country and searching out insects on the ground. Pesticides have killed off many of these insects and so put the lesser kestrel at risk.

Falcons that live in forests suffer badly when the trees are cut down. On the island of Mauritius, in the Indian

Lesser kestrels spend the summer in southern Europe and central Asia. They fly to Africa for the winter, where their habitat is facing the same problems as in Europe.

Ocean, lives the Mauritius kestrel. About 10 inches (25 cm) long, this kestrel has a red-brown back and head, with white underparts blotched with brown or black. It sometimes hunts birds by chasing them through its thick forest home. Its wings are shorter and more rounded than those of most falcons, so it can dodge between the trees.

The Mauritius kestrel was almost wiped out by logging, which destroyed its nesting trees and took away its food supply. By 1974 there were only six Mauritius kestrels left! Scientists brought some eggs into **captivity**, where European kestrels **incubated** them and raised the chicks. The young birds were then released back into the wild. This helped build up numbers, and in 1996 there were about 350 Mauritius kestrels in the world.

A Mauritius kestrel settles down to a meal. These kestrels eat insects, small birds, and small lizards called geckos. This bird is fitted with a radio set so its movements can be tracked.

An osprey with a freshly caught fish in Florida. An adult osprey can catch fish of up to 4 pounds (2 kg), which is more than the bird itself weighs.

Hawks

As we have seen, hawks can be divided into a number of groups. Each of these has its own hunting method. Some hawks hunt by soaring high above open ground. Others catch their prey by ambushing it in dense woodland. In this section, we will take a look at a wide variety of hawks, beginning with the osprey, a fish-eating hawk.

Ospreys

The osprey is a big bird, about 22 inches (56 cm) long, with a dark brown back, white underparts, and a white head with a dark streak on either side of its bright yellow eyes. It is found all over the world, yet it always looks the same. This makes it easy to recognize – especially when it is looking for food.

Ospreys nearly always hunt over the open water of large rivers and lakes or along coasts. A hunting osprey flies slowly above the water. If it sees a fish, it plunges toward the surface with its wings half-closed and its talons outstretched, splashing down in a cloud of spray. Moments later it reappears, usually with a big, juicy fish clutched in

An osprey struggles to take off, carrying its meal. The osprey has specially adapted talons that give it a firm grip on its slippery prey.

its talons. It struggles into the air, shakes the water from its feathers, and flies off to a favorite perch to eat its meal.

Ospreys usually nest near water, often in tall trees, in which they build huge nests of sticks and branches. A pair of ospreys usually comes back to the same place each season. Year after year, the birds repair the nest, which grows bigger and bigger. These large nests are easy to find, and this helped put the osprey in danger.

In the past many people collected birds' eggs. An osprey's egg was a rare prize, and since the nests were so easy to see, the eggs were often stolen. This became a serious problem for ospreys in Scotland, where they were

Areas where the osprey can be found

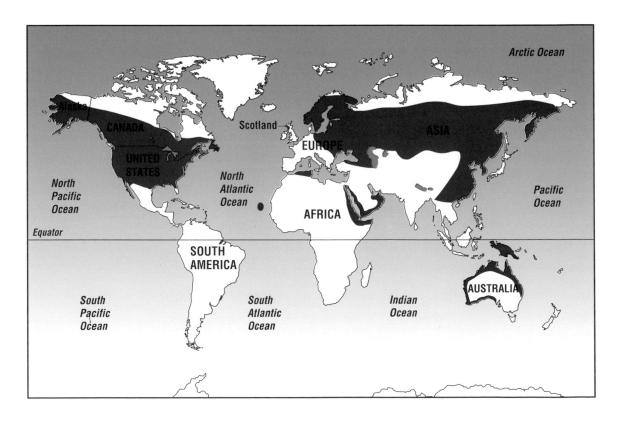

already being shot to stop them from eating valuable salmon. By 1903 the osprey had vanished from Scotland, and the same thing happened elsewhere in Europe.

Ospreys in North America, like peregrines, have suffered from pesticide poisoning. Farm chemicals were draining into lakes and rivers, where they got into the fish that ospreys eat. By the early 1960s ospreys were disappearing from many parts of the northeastern United States.

Today the chemicals that caused the trouble are no longer used in the United States, and osprey numbers are increasing. Meanwhile, ospreys have returned to Scotland, where the birds and their eggs are now strictly protected. Although ospreys are still shot and poisoned in some parts of the world, the bird is making a comeback and is no longer on the danger list.

An osprey perches on a tall cactus as it watches over its magnificent nest in Baja California, Mexico.

Cooper's hawk is a North American forest hawk that feeds mainly on birds such as flickers and thrushes.

Forest Hawks

Some hawks are specialized forest hunters. They have short wings with rounded tips so they can fly easily between the trees. They also have long tails to help them steer through the tangled branches. Instead of patrolling the skies in search of prey, forest hawks often perch in the shadows, waiting to ambush other birds as they fly past. They burst from cover and chase their prey at high speed, zigzagging between the trees before striking with their talons.

There are many different species of forest hawks, and they are found all over the world. Small ones like the

Eurasian sparrowhawk and the American sharp-shinned hawk prey mainly on small birds. Bigger ones like the North American Cooper's hawk often pluck squirrels from the branches. The biggest of all, like the northern goshawk (GOSS-hawk), are powerful enough to kill young hares.

A northern goshawk is a magnificent bird. Up to 26 inches (66 cm) long, it has a pale breast barred with dark brown, a dark brown back, and red-yellow eyes that seem to stare. It is found in northern forests all around the globe, from North America eastward to Siberia. Females are much bigger than males and able to kill big **gamebirds** such as pheasants. This made goshawks unpopular with hunters, who like to shoot gamebirds, and they killed many

Some forest hawks live in or near cities, where they meet unexpected dangers. This Eurasian sparrowhawk was killed as it chased a dove into a glass door that it did not see.

goshawks. Goshawks have also suffered from pesticide poisoning and **pollution**. Although these birds are difficult to count, numbers of goshawks have certainly fallen in parts of their **range**. Even so, this amazing forest hunter is not in danger of becoming extinct.

Falconers use goshawks. Most of these are bred in captivity. Since goshawks are valuable, though, some dealers steal eggs and young birds from wild nests and pretend they have been captive-bred. Today scientists can check whether a bird is wild or not by testing its blood. This practice may help to stop the illegal trade in wild goshawks and other birds of prey, such as peregrines.

Hawks have also been killed by people because they sometimes feed on domestic chickens. Cooper's hawk, for

An unlucky moorhen has fallen prey to a female northern goshawk. The hawk hunches over its meal to shield it from rivals.

example, has suffered for this reason. Nicknamed the "chicken hawk" because of its liking for chickens, Cooper's is a medium-sized forest hawk. It has a gray back and whitish underparts barred with rusty red and can be found in forests over most of the United States and Canada. North American farmers killed so many Cooper's hawks that numbers fell. Today, it is against federal law to kill hawks in the United States, and numbers have started to increase again.

Gundlach's hawk has also been hunted because it likes to eat chickens. Gundlach's is closely related to Cooper's hawk and looks very similar. It lives only on the Caribbean island of Cuba and is in great danger of becoming extinct.

Areas where the northern goshawk can be found

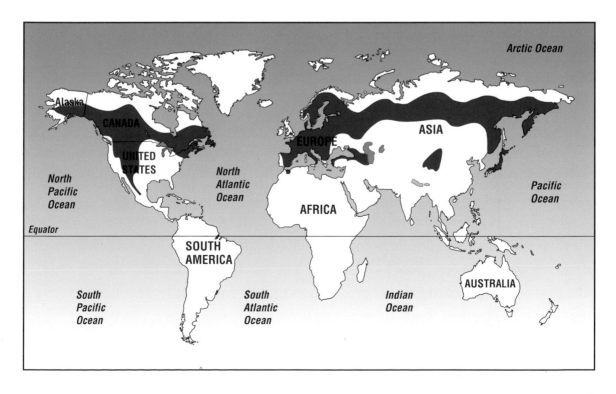

UNITED STATES

Florida

North
Atlantic
Ocean

CUBA

South
Pacific
Ocean

SOUTH
AMERICA

Area where
Gundlach's hawk
can be found

Not only is Gundlach's hawk killed as a pest to farmers but it is also losing its forest habitat.

The loss of their woodland homes is the biggest problem facing forest hawks today. Like all hunters, hawks are naturally scarce compared to the animals they eat. So while a forest may provide a home for thousands of small birds, it will contain only a handful of the hawks that eat them. If most of the forest is cut down, many small birds will survive. But birds of prey usually die out because there are too few of them to breed, and their favorite nesting sites have disappeared. If Gundlach's hawk is to survive, areas of Cuban forest must be preserved. And the killing of this bird as a pest needs to be stopped.

Cooper's hawk – seen here with young – is very similar to Gundlach's hawk. Scientists know little about Gundlach's hawk besides the fact that it is very rare.

Harriers

While falcons and forest hawks have perfected the high-speed attack, harriers have developed a very different way of hunting. Instead of chasing other birds through the air, these hawks fly slowly and low over open country such as grassland or marsh, looking and listening for small animals like mice and frogs. Gliding on outstretched wings, often less than 10 feet (3 m) above the ground, a harrier surprises its victim by suddenly appearing just overhead. It then pounces on the helpless creature with its sharp talons.

Like all hawks, northern harriers have amazing eyesight, but like owls they also have great hearing.

During the breeding season, male harriers often show off to females by "skydancing." The bird flies to about 100 feet (30 m) above the ground, somersaults, and then dives straight downward. Just before he reaches the ground, he pulls up and begins the dance over again. Sometimes the female joins in. At other times she watches from a perch.

Unlike most other birds of prey, male and female harriers look quite different. The male northern harrier, for example, is pale gray with white underparts, while the female has a dark brown back and creamy underparts with brown streaks. Found throughout much of Europe, northern Asia, and North America, where it is often known as the "marsh hawk," the northern harrier grows to about 20 inches (50 cm) long. The marsh harrier of Europe, Asia,

A female northern harrier blends in well among the reeds as she shades her young from the sun.

and Australia is even larger, growing to 23 inches (58 cm) long. The male has pale gray wings and tail, while the female is chocolate brown with a cream-colored head.

Female harriers tend to be less brightly colored than males, because they usually incubate the eggs and guard the young while the male hunts for food. Most harriers nest on the ground in the cover of reeds or long grass, so the female needs to have dull colors to keep hidden from enemies. When the male returns from a hunting trip, the female often flies up to him, turning upside-down in midair to catch the food in her talons.

In some places the voles (small mouselike creatures) that harriers eat may be scarce at times, so many harrier chicks

Areas where the northern harrier can be found

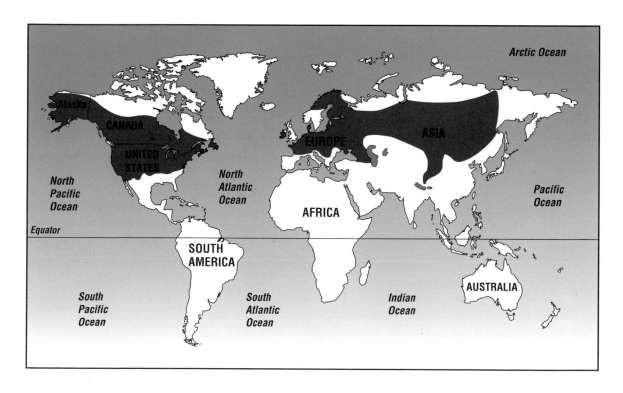

starve to death in the nest. In other years the opposite happens: there is so much food that more harriers survive than usual. This means that harrier numbers go up and down all the time. This is natural and has happened for thousands of years without putting these birds at risk.

However, harriers cannot get used to the shortages created by people. As more rough grassland is plowed up and more marshes are drained, harriers are left with fewer places to live. They are also killed by hunters and by gamekeepers trying to protect gamebirds. And where harriers nest in fields, the chicks are sometimes accidentally crushed to death by tractors. All this has led to the northern harrier being put at risk in Europe, along with the closely related and very similar pallid harrier. Harriers are not as threatened as many hawks, but they are far from safe.

A marsh harrier flies low over the reeds. Like many marshland birds, it has suffered from habitat loss, but so far is not in danger.

The black kite is a fearless bird that will snatch food from market stalls and even out of people's hands.

Kites

Some hawks and falcons are easily recognized by the way they behave. As we have seen, kestrels usually hunt by hovering in midair, while harriers fly slowly near the ground. But the kites include a wide variety of birds with quite different habits.

The black kite, for example, will eat almost anything, from wild birds to kitchen scraps. Found over a huge area from Europe to Australia, black kites are a common sight in Asian cities where they feed on scraps and leftovers in

Areas where the red kite can be found

the streets. This ability to live near people and to eat a wide variety of food has kept the black kite off the danger list.

The closely related red kite shares the black kite's diet, but is far less willing to come into contact with people. A big, beautiful bird up to 24 inches (61 cm) in length, with a long, forked tail and rust color, it lives mainly in the wooded, hilly areas of Europe. It has suffered badly from hunting and the loss of its habitat and is no longer found in many parts of its range. In Britain, where it almost disappeared, the red kite is now protected, and numbers have increased to more than 120 birds. However, illegal killing still goes on, and the red kite is not safe yet.

The forked tail of the rare red kite makes it easy to recognize as it flies over its hilly home. It is believed that the kites people fly get their name from this graceful bird.

Some species of kites do not have varied diets but feed on one particular food. One of these is the snail kite, which is found in South and Central America as well as in the Everglades of Florida. This kite grows to 18 inches (46 cm) long and is another of the birds of prey in which the male and female look different. The male bird is blackish gray with a white band in its tail, while the female has a brown back and streaky white and brown underparts.

The snail kite feeds entirely on small freshwater snails, called apple snails, which it finds by flying low over marshland. When it spots a snail it drops, feet first, toward the water. It snatches up its prey and flies off with it to a perch, where it eats its catch.

A red kite settles on top of a telephone pole with its prey. One reason that farmers killed this beautiful bird was that it stole domestic chickens.

Areas where the
snail kite can be
found

In Florida, the snail kite is now rare, mainly because of human disturbance of the Everglades. Marshland was drained for farmland and homes, and farm chemicals and pesticides flowed into the swamps. Many tourists also visited the area, disturbing nesting birds. By 1970, **conservationists** believed that only about ten snail kites survived. To protect these birds, the public were kept out of the parts of the Everglades where snail kites were nesting. As a result, the number of snail kites has increased. However, only by permanently setting aside large areas of snail kite habitat will the bird's future be safe.

A snail kite at a feeding perch. Snail kites often go back to the same place to eat, and piles of up to 200 snail shells have been found beneath perches.

Many of the threats that once faced hawks and falcons are lessening. For example, scientists are trying to replace poisonous chemicals with safer ones. This is partly because people are learning to value the beauty and wonder of wildlife. It is also because scientists realize that chemicals damaging to birds are probably harmful to us, too.

But all wild creatures and plants are still at risk when forests and wilderness areas are destroyed, and hawks and falcons are among the first to disappear. We need to make sure they survive by saving what is left of their natural habitats. If we do this, we will also be providing a future for the other animals and plants that make up their world.

The snail kite's hooked, needlelike bill is adapted for cutting snails from their shells.

Useful Addresses

For more information about hawks and falcons and how you can help protect them, contact these organizations:

Birds of Prey Rehabilitation Foundation
RR 2, Box 659
Broomfield, CO 80020

Hawk Mountain Sanctuary Association
RR 2, Box 191
Kempton, PA 19529-9449

International Council for Bird Preservation
P.O. Box 57242
Washington, D.C. 20037-7242

Peregrine Fund
World Center for Birds of Prey
5666 W. Flying Hawk Lane
Boise, Idaho 83709

U.S. Fish and Wildlife Service
Endangered Species and Habitat
Conservation
400 Arlington Square
18th and C Streets NW
Washington, D.C. 20240

World Wildlife Fund
1250 24th Street NW
Washington, D.C. 20037

World Wildlife Fund Canada
90 Eglinton Avenue East
Suite 504
Toronto
Ontario M4P 2Z7

Further Reading

Bird David Burnie (New York: Knopf, 1988)

Eagles, Hawks and Other Birds of Prey Lynda De Witt (New York: Franklin Watts, 1989)

Endangered Wildlife of the World (New York: Marshall Cavendish Corporation, 1993)

Falcons and Hawks Dr Penny Owen (Sydney: Weldon Owen Pty Ltd, 1992)

Saving Endangered Birds: Ensuring a Future in the Wild Thane Maynard (New York: Franklin Watts, 1993)

The Usborne Book of Bird Facts Bridget Gibbs (London: Usborne Pub. Ltd, 1990)

Wildlife of the World (New York: Marshall Cavendish Corporation, 1994)

Glossary

Adapt: To change in order to survive in new conditions.

Bird of prey: A type of bird that usually has a hooked bill and clawed feet and hunts and eats other animals.

Captivity: Confinement; for birds, usually in a cage.

Conservationist (Kon-ser-VAY-shun-ist): A person who protects and preserves the Earth's natural resources, such as animals, plants, and soil.

Extinct (Ex-TINKT): No longer living anywhere in the world.

Falconers: People who keep hawks and falcons and sometimes use them to hunt other animals.

Gamebirds: Pheasants, turkeys, and similar birds that are often bred to be shot for sport.

Gamekeepers: People who breed and raise gamebirds.

Habitat: The place where an animal lives. For example, the northern goshawk's habitat is the forest.

Incubate (IN-kyew-bait): In birds, to sit on eggs in order to keep them warm so they will hatch.

Pesticides (PES-ti-sides): Chemicals used to kill insects, other animals, and diseases that damage crops or animals.

Pollution (Puh-LOO-shun): Materials, such as garbage, fumes, and chemicals, that damage the environment.

Prey: An animal that is hunted and eaten by another animal.

Range: The area in the world in which a particular kind of animal can be found.

Species: A kind of animal or plant. For example, the lesser kestrel is a species of falcon.

Talons: Curved claws of a bird of prey.

Tropical: Having to do with or found in the tropics, the warm region of the Earth near the Equator. For example, tropical rainforest.

Index

CHRISTMAS CARD CUT-OUTS FROM MAGAZINES

What You Need: old magazines or old Christmas cards (*and* permission to cut pictures out of them), scissors, glue, coloured felt tip or pencil.

Optional: glitter, ribbon, and material.

What You Do:

1. Look through the magazines or cards for a picture that you like. You may find pictures of Father Christmas, or a child playing in the snow, or a beautifully wrapped gift. When you find the right picture, cut it out.

2. Glue the picture onto your card.

Optional:

3. Draw in your own picture around the cut-out. For example, if you cut out a picture of a Christmas tree, you could draw a picture of a snowy forest, or your town, or your living room, around it.

4. Decorate your card with glitter or small pieces of material or ribbon.

CHRISTMAS PHOTOGRAPHS

What You Need: a photograph of yourself (*and* permission to cut it up), scissors, glue, pencil, coloured felt tips or pencils. (Note: You could have a picture taken especially for this card, and make as many copies of the photo as you need for the number of people you want to give it to. *It takes time to have film developed and reprints made.* Ask an adult for help.)

Optional: glitter, ribbon, material, magazine cut-outs.

What You Do:

1. Once you have the photograph, decide how you want it shown on your card. You could:
   Cut your whole self out of the photograph and place it on the front cover.
   Or cut a small circle out of the front cover. Glue your photograph on the inside, so that your face shows through the hole in front.
   Or cut out a picture from a magazine and stick your own picture on it. (This would make a very funny card.) For example, if you cut out a picture of a snowman, you could cut your head out of your photograph and put it where the snowman's head would be.

There are many creative ways to include your picture in a Christmas card.

2. Print your Christmas message in pencil, then go over it in coloured felt tip or pencil.

Optional:

3. Decorate your card with glitter, ribbon, or material.

HOW TO MAKE CHRISTMAS GIFTS

Tony Cenicola

Pin Cushion

This is an ideal gift for anyone who sews.

What you need: a polystyrene or sponge ball (about the size of a medium tomato), a piece of pretty cotton fabric that's large enough to fit easily over the ball, a long piece (about 30 centimetres [12 inches]) of wool or ribbon, and scissors.

What You Do:

1. Place the polystyrene ball in the centre of the fabric.

2. Bring the fabric up over the ball and gather all the ends together.

3. Tie the fabric ends tightly together with wool or ribbon.

4. Snip the ends of the wool or ribbon, if they're too long.

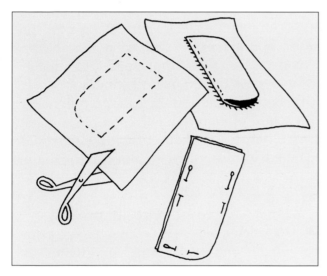

Trace the shape of the spectacles case on two pieces of felt. Cut around the outline and pin the two pieces together before sewing.

Felt Eyeglasses Case

If you know how to sew, this is a useful gift to make. For someone who wears glasses, an extra storage case is always handy.

What You Need: one borrowed glasses case, two pieces of felt at least 18 centimetres long x 9 centimetres wide (7 inches long x 3½ inches), pen or pencil, needle, thread, scissors, and other small bits of material to sew on as decoration, and glue.

What You Do:

1. Place the borrowed eyeglasses case on a piece of felt and trace around the edges with a pencil.

2. Repeat this step with a second piece of felt.

3. Carefully cut out the outlines on the two pieces of felt.

4. Match the two pieces, and pin together the edges of the two long and one of the short sides with dressmaker's pins.

5. While the felt is still pinned around the edges, test to see whether a pair of glasses will fit into your case. Slide them in gently. If the case is too small, start over. If it's too big, either trim the edges with scissors, or plan to sew your stitches further in from the edge.

6. With needle and thread, stitch up the two long sides and one short side of the case.

7. You can decorate the case by cutting small shapes from felt or other fabric, such as a flower or the initials of the person you're giving it to. Then simply glue them on. Let the glue dry.

8. If you borrowed someone else's glasses and glasses case, be sure to return them.

Tie your book together with pretty pieces of ribbon.

A Book, By You!

If you like to write stories or poems, create your own book, which will become a treasured gift.

What You Need: rough paper (for practicing your story), pen, nice white paper, coloured card, stapler or hole puncher, ribbon or wool, scissors, glue.

Optional: (to illustrate your book): coloured pencils or felt tips, pictures from magazines, or pieces of material.

What You Do:

1. Make up a short story, or write out a favourite tale you know. (There are good ones in this book.) Write your story on rough paper first, as practice.

2. Write your story again on nice white paper. If you wish to illustrate your book, save room on the pages for your pictures.

Optional:

3. For a fancier look, write out your story on strips of nice white paper and glue each strip onto a larger piece of coloured card. If you wish to illustrate, save room on the coloured card for your picture.

Optional:

4. Here are three other ways to illustrate your story:

    a. with felt tips or coloured pencils;

    b. with pictures cut out of magazines;

    c. with scraps of material or bright paper. (For example, you could make a house and garden with three pieces of material: a triangle set on top of a square or rectangle for the house, and a narrow strip of material with several cuts in it for the grass. Cut smaller rectangles for the doors and windows.)

It's also possible to mix your own drawing with scraps of material. For example, a piece of material in the shape of a triangle could become a girl's skirt, when glued to the drawing.

5. Make a book cover. Here are two ways:

    a. On a clean, separate piece of paper, print the title of your book, and your name, as author.

    b. On a large, clean piece of paper, create an illustration. Write the title and name of the author (you) on a smaller, separate strip of paper. Glue the strip onto the cover.

6. Gather together the cover and pages of your book. Bind them together in order on the left-hand side in either of the following ways:

    a. Staple the pages together at the top, middle, and bottom of the left edge. Glue a pretty strip of ribbon over the staples.

    b. Punch holes on each page at the top, middle, and bottom of the left edge, one sheet at a time. Try to have the holes in the same place on each page. Bind the pages together by threading bright wool or ribbon through the holes and tying the ends in a knot.

Telephone Pad

What You Need: pad of paper, either 13 centimetres x 20 centimetres, or 10 centimetres x 15 centimetres (approximately 5 inches x 8 inches, or 4 inches x 6 inches); two pieces of stiff card (both pieces the same size, and each a little bigger than the pad of paper); glue, and scissors. To decorate: your choice of coloured felt tips, felt or other pieces of material, or poster paints.

Glue the pad of paper to a sturdy backing.

What You Do:

1. Put your pad of paper on a larger piece of stiff card. Cut out two pieces, one to cover the top of the pad and the other to cover the bottom.

2. Glue one piece of stiff card to the bottom of the pad. Glue the other piece to the top of the pad, for the cover.

3. Decorate the cover with any of the materials suggested above.

Decorate the top with a fanciful drawing.

© Christopher Bain 1988

Personalized Shop-Bought Gifts

You can add a personal, homemade touch to many gifts that you buy in shops to make those presents extra special. Here are some suggestions:

Decorated Waste Paper Baskets

What You Need: plastic or metal waste paper basket, sticky back plastic, glue, scissors. Optional: different coloured pieces of felt, or other pretty pieces of material, ribbon.

What You Do:

1. Using the sticky back plastic, cut out the design with which you wish to cover your waste paper basket. Your design could be Christmas related, like a snowman or Christmas tree; or it could be a design that would be appropriate all year round, like flowers, boats, trains, or whatever you like best.

2. Peel the back of the sticky back plastic off your cut-outs and stick each piece onto the waste paper basket.

Optional:

3. Glue a piece of ribbon around the top and bottom of the waste paper basket.

4. If you do not use sticky back plastic, you could make cut-outs from other sorts of material like fabric. Apply glue to the back of each piece and stick it on the waste paper basket. Make sure you let the glue dry.

Gifts With Painted Messages

On the outside bottom of a mug, bowl, plate, or pottery jar, there's room to paint a message like, "To Mum, Love from Your Favourite Christmas Elf, Eliza!"

What you need: newspapers, pencil, acrylic paint (not water-colours), thin-tipped paintbrush, and a cup of water.

What You Do:

1. Spread out the newspapers over your work space.

2. Lightly write your message in pencil on the bottom of your gift. If you make a mistake, you can rub it out and try again. If pencil does not show up, practice writing your message on a piece of rough paper to make sure it will fit on your gift.

3. Write the message on your gift in paint.

4. When finished painting, keep your gift turned upside down, so the paint can dry.

Painted Gardening Gloves

What You Need: a pair of plain, canvas gloves (available at most hardware shops), paper, pencil, newspaper, acrylic paint, and medium-sized paintbrush.

What You Do:

1. With a pencil and a piece of rough paper, work out the design you wish to paint on your gloves. Try to keep your design simple, because there is not much room on the glove for detailed pictures. It will also be easier to paint.

2. Spread out newspaper over your work space.

3. With paintbrush and acrylic paints, paint your design on one glove, then the other. Because canvas is a rough surface, it may be necessary to go over your design more than once.

4. Let the gloves dry.

Painted Flowerpot

What You Need: a clay or plastic flowerpot (available at a hardware or department store), poster or acrylic paint, newspaper, medium-sized paintbrush, paper, and pencil.

What You Do:

1. With a piece of paper and pencil, work out the design for your flowerpot. You can put a simple design or picture on one part of the pot, or you can carry the design all the way around.

2. Spread newspapers over your work space.

3. Paint the flowerpot, using your plan on paper to guide you.

4. Let the paint dry.

You can paint a cheerful picture or pattern on a flowerpot.

Photograph Key Ring

Your parents will love seeing a picture of you and your family on their key ring, every time they start the car or lock the front door.

What You Need: one key ring with a small, clear plastic or lucite frame attached (available at hardware or stationery shops), a picture that fits the key ring frame, scissors.

What You Do:

1. Find a few photographs that you think may fit the small clear frame. If the pictures do not belong to you, make sure that you have permission to take them and that no one wants the pictures back.

2. Take the pictures to a hardware or stationery shop, where a shop assistant will help you pick out a key ring.

3. You may have to cut off some of the photo to fit the frame—that's alright. And make sure the photo is secure in the key ring before giving it as a gift.

Framed Picture

What You Need: a nice picture that you drew or an especially nice picture that you coloured or painted from a book, and a picture frame (available at most department stores).

Optional: coloured card or stiff card.

What You Do:

1. Measure the size of the picture you wish to frame.

2. Take your picture, or just its measurements, with you when you go to the shop to buy your frame. Pick the frame that will fit best.

3. If your picture is too big for the frame in the nearest size, you may need to trim the edges of your picture. If the picture is too small, choose a colourful piece of coloured card or stiff card that fits neatly inside the frame. Sellotape your picture to that, then place the coloured card inside the frame.

© Christopher Bain 1988

Framed Photograph

This is for those with a camera. Many chemist and photo shops can develop film in a day, sometimes less. If you wish to get the picture enlarged (made bigger), however, it may take more time.

What You Need: a nice photograph of either yourself or other family members (if the gift is for someone in your family), and a picture frame to fit the picture (available at most department stores).

What You Do:

1. Have someone take photos of you, or take a few pictures of the people you would like to put in your frame.

2. Get the film developed at any chemist or photo shop.

3. When the pictures come back, pick the one you like best. If you have the time and extra money, perhaps the picture would look good enlarged. The most common sizes for enlargements are 13 centimetres x 17 centimetres (5 inches x 7 inches), and 20 centimetres x 25 centimetres (8 inches x 10 inches). Ask the shop assistant at a camera shop to show you the different sizes.

4. Buy the frame in the proper size for your picture. Department stores have many sorts of frames, and the sizes are printed on the outside packaging.

Tony Cenicola

How to Wrap Christmas Gifts

Wrapping gifts is a nice way of showing someone that you care about the gift you are giving. It does not have to take a long time, and it should be fun. Have an adult help you the first time, until you get the knack.

Knowing how to cut the piece of paper to the right size and how to fold it around your gift will make wrapping much easier, and give you more time to decorate it later. Follow the instructions below to learn how to wrap a normal-sized gift in a box. The next section will discuss different ways to wrap odd-shaped presents.

I. Wrapping Basics

What You Need: a roll or large sheet of wrapping paper, scissors, sellotape, a ruler.

What You Do:

1. After you've opened your wrapping paper, you may notice that there is a plain side (the "inside") and a coloured or decorated side (the "outside").

2. Look at your box. There is a top, a bottom, and four sides. To cut a piece of wrapping paper the correct size, place your present so the *top* of the box is face-down on the inside of the wrapping paper 5–8 centimetres (2–3 inches) in from the edge of the paper.

3. Bring the rest of the paper over the gift, until it meets up with the edge.

4. Make a crease in the paper where it meets the edge. Cut along the crease to the end of the paper.

You should now have a piece of paper that easily covers the top, bottom, and all sides of the box. The next steps will explain how to cut and fold the paper around the box.

5. Centre your present on the piece of wrapping paper, with its top side down. There should be an equal amount of paper on the left and right sides of the box.

6. Check the ends of the paper to make sure there is enough to cover the ends of your box. To do that, take a ruler and measure how high the box is; then measure how much paper there is at either end. For example: If the box is 2½ centimetres (one inch) high, there should be about 5 centimetres (2 inches) of paper at either end.

If one end is too short, simply move the box.

If one end is too long, take your scissors and trim the paper until it is the right size.

7. Now bring both sides of the paper up tightly, to the centre of the top of the box. Put one side down over the other. Hold them together with one hand.

8. With the other hand, take a piece of sellotape and stick it on the box so that it holds both sides of the paper together. (Putting the sellotape on sideways will hold the paper together best.)

9. Add two or three more pieces of sellotape, so the paper on the box is held together securely.

10. With your thumbs, gently press one end of paper down against the edges of the box to crease it. This will make it easier to fold down the corners of the paper.

11. Take one corner and bring it up to the end side of the box. Press the corner fold down.

12. Do the same thing with the other corner. What you have now is a flap of paper at one end, which looks like an upside down triangle, its point facing you.

13. Bring the point of that triangle up the side to the top of the box and tape it down securely.

14. Now turn the box around and follow the same steps (11–14) for the other end.

Your gift should now be wrapped and ready to decorate.

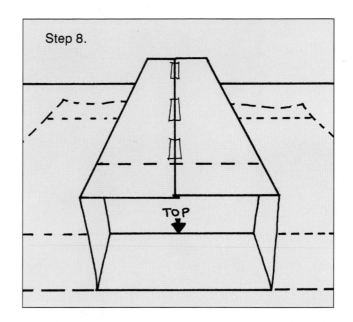

Step 8.

TOP

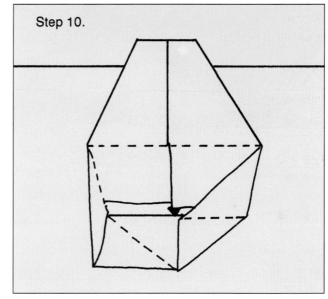

Step 10.

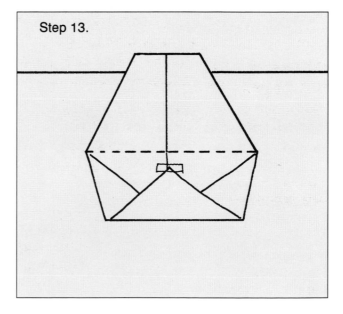

Step 13.

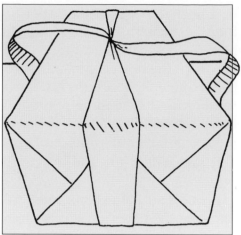

Tony Cenicola

II. How To Tie a Ribbon

Ribbons are a pretty way to complete the wrapping of a gift. Ribbons come in many different materials, sizes, and colours, but the easiest way of tying them around a gift is the same. Here's how you do it:

1. Take a long piece of ribbon. The ribbon should be long enough to be wrapped both lengthwise and widthwise around your gift.

2. The top of your gift should be facing up. With both hands holding onto the ribbon, slip it underneath the gift. Bring the ribbon up and around the gift, and even out the two ends until each of your hands is holding the same amount of ribbon.

3. Now, exchange ribbons: Take the ribbon in your right hand and give it to your left hand. Then take the ribbon in your left hand and give it to your right hand. When the ribbons are held up together, they should form an "X".

4. Bring the ribbons down and around your gift making a cross on the top.

5. Turn the gift upside down and tie the two ribbons together in a knot on the bottom. Snip the extra ribbon with scissors.

6. Take another piece of ribbon. This piece should be long enough to tie a bow, but give yourself a little extra ribbon, just in case.

7. Place your gift right side up, and slip the new ribbon under the cross.

III. How To Wrap Oddly-Shaped Gifts

Some gifts come in odd shapes and don't seem to fit into any available box. Here are some different ways to wrap those difficult gifts.

TISSUE PAPER GIFT WRAP

Tissue paper is very flexible, even when it's several layers thick. For that reason, it is easy to work with and good for wrapping odd-shaped gifts.

What You Need: tissue paper, scissors, ribbon.

What You Do:

1. Roll your gift up in tissue paper as best as you can. Make sure all the sharp angles are covered. Your gift may look odd—that's alright.

2. Once all the sharp angles are covered up with the first wrapping, you may want to add a second layer of wrapping. This time, try wrapping as closely as possible to the traditional method explained on page 64.

3. Tie a ribbon around your gift.

4. Add a Christmas gift tag.

Tony Cencicola

COFFEE TIN, PAIL, OR FLOWERPOT GIFT WRAP

What You Need: an empty coffee tin, pail, flowerpot, or similar container; tissue paper, ribbon, scissors, lightweight wrapping paper.

What You Do:

1. Put a layer or two of tissue paper inside your container, for decoration. It's alright if some of the paper sticks out of the container.

2. Crumple some more tissue paper and stick it in the bottom of the container. Crumpled paper will help cushion your gift and prevent it from breaking.

3. Put your gift inside the container. (You may wish to roll some tissue paper around your gift before doing so.)

4. Fill the rest of the container up with tissue paper, until your gift is completely covered.

5. Spread out a large sheet of wrapping paper, with the coloured or patterned side facing down. The paper should be large enough to cover your container, plus a little extra; or, spread out several layers of fresh tissue paper over your work space.

6. Put your container in the middle of the paper with the top facing up.

7. Cut a long piece of ribbon and set it aside.

8. Bring all sides of the paper up over the centre of the container.

9. Tie the paper sides together at the top with the ribbon.

10. Tie a bow with the ribbon, and add a Christmas gift tag.

Tony Cenicola

CARRIER BAG GIFT WRAP

What You Need: one paper carrier bag, tissue paper, scissors, sellotape or stapler, ribbon.

What You Do:

1. Roll tissue paper around your gift. (This is mostly for decoration.)

2. Lightly crumple some more tissue paper and put it at the bottom of your carrier bag. Keep adding tissue paper, until the bottom of the bag looks fluffy. Make sure there is enough paper in the bag to protect your gift from breaking.

3. Place your gift inside the bag.

4. Add some more slightly crumpled tissue paper on top of your gift.

5. Seal the bag shut with sellotape, or with a stapler.

6. For decoration, add ribbons to the carrier bag handles. For more ideas on how to decorate your bag, see the suggestions on pages 70 and 71.

7. Add a Christmas gift tag.

PAPER CONE GIFT WRAP

This sort of wrapping is best with small, lightweight gifts.

What You Need: one piece of rectangular-shaped wrapping paper, sellotape, tissue paper.

What You Do:

1. Spread your wrapping paper out on your work space, with the inside of the paper facing upward.

2. Turn your paper so that the longer sides are on the top and bottom.

3. Using both hands, bring the bottom corners together toward the centre and overlap one over the other. Do not fold the paper!

4. Pull the outside corner until the cone is the size you want.

5. Tape the outside corner to the cone.

6. Roll your present in tissue paper.

7. Stuff tissue paper or cotton wool into the bottom of the cone.

8. Place your gift in the cone.

9. Cover your present with more tissue paper or cotton wool.

10. Add a Christmas gift tag.

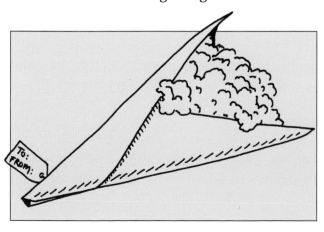

IV. How To Make Christmas Gift Tags

No gift is complete until you include a small card or tag saying whom the gift is for and whom it is from. These tags are sold in shops along with gift wrapping and ribbons. It is also possible to make gift tags yourself. Here's how:

What You Need: a small scrap of wrapping paper, scissors and/or pinking shears, sellotape or thread.

What You Do:

1. Cut the scrap of wrapping paper into a square.

2. Fold the piece of paper in half with the undecorated or uncoloured side on the inside. If necessary, trim the sides.

3. Your piece of paper should now open like a little book. On the inside, write the name of the person receiving the gift, and then, of course, write your own name as the giver. For example, "To Granny, Love, Michael."

4. To attach the tag, put a tiny hole at the top right hand corner. Slip a thread through the hole and tie it onto the ribbon wrapped around the gift. OR: Sellotape the card to your gift. Use either double-sided or regular, sellotape on the back.

Other Suggestions:

1. Make your tag a different shape: a circle, triangle, or even a Christmas tree. To do this, fold the wrapping paper in half, as explained earlier. Then cut out the shape you want—but be sure not to cut the fold. The fold holds the card together.

2. If your paper has an interesting pattern, fold your paper so the whole picture shows. Then cut around the picture—but remember not to cut the fold.

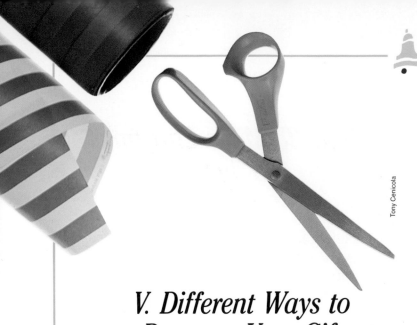

Tony Cenicola

V. Different Ways to Decorate Your Gift

Tying a simple ribbon and bow on a gift makes it pretty. But with a little extra time and thought, your present can have a personal touch, which makes the person receiving your gift feel special. Remember, though, not to spend *too* much time decorating your gift, since your wrapping will probably not be saved. Just make decorating fun for yourself and the results will be good—and appreciated by the recipient of your gift.

The following are ways to make your wrapping unique:

CHRISTMAS CUT-OUTS

What You Need: plain wrapping paper, patterned wrapping paper, ribbon, scissors, sellotape.

What You Do:

1. Find wrapping paper with a fun pattern on it for your cut-out. Large prints are usually easiest to work with.

2. Wrap your gift in plain wrapping paper—but one that will go well with the patterned wrapping paper.

3. Tie a single ribbon, or two ribbons around your parcel. You may want to add a bow, but it's not necessary.

4. Cut out the pattern from the patterned wrapping paper. You can cut it out with plain scissors or pinking shears, for a zigzag edge.

Try all sorts of shapes, such as animals, houses, and people to make your wrapping paper unique. It's not always necessary to cut the pattern out perfectly; sometimes simply cutting *around* the pattern and including some of the background works just as well. You decide what would look best on your parcel, and how much time you want to spend cutting.

5. Place the cut-out on the parcel where you think it looks best, and sellotape it down. Perhaps one cut-out does not seem like enough. In that case, add more cut-outs. You can sellotape them anywhere on the parcel, or sellotape them all along the ribbon. Or, if you have tied a bow in the centre, try placing cut-outs on either side of it.

PICTURES FROM MAGAZINES AND CHRISTMAS CARDS

What You Need: pictures from magazines and Christmas cards (get your parents' permission to cut them up), scissors, sellotape.

Optional: ribbon.

What You Do:

1. Go through the magazines or Christmas cards and look for a picture or photograph that you like. You might find some nice Christmas pictures, or a photograph that gives a little hint about what's inside your gift; or it might be just a funny illustration or cartoon that both you and the person receiving your gift will enjoy.

2. Cut the picture out.

3. Decide where to put the picture on your parcel. Stick the picture on with sellotape. (Using glue takes more time and can get messy.)

4. You could also frame the picture with ribbon. You can either tie the ribbon around your parcel to frame it, or cut and tape the ribbon to fit the edges of the picture.

CHRISTMAS TREE

What You Need: wrapping paper, scissors, sellotape.

Optional: light-coloured card and pen.

What You Do:

1. Choose a wrapping paper that will go well with the paper in which you wrapped your gift.

2. Cut out a Christmas tree shape from the wrapping paper.

3. Sellotape it on your gift.

Optional:

4. From light-coloured card, cut out a large star or Christmas tree ornament and sellotape it to the top of the Christmas tree.

5. Use the star or ornament as a Christmas gift tag, which says whom the gift is for and whom it is from.

CHRISTMAS TREE ORNAMENT

What To Do:

1. Make one of the Christmas tree ornaments in the section that starts on page 74.

2. Attach your ornament to your parcel. One way you can do this is by tying your ornament onto the ribbon around your gift. Loop wool or ribbon through the hole in your ornament and make a knot to hold it onto your package. Or use sellotape to stick your ornament on. (Sellotape works best with flat, lightweight ornaments.)

You can make Father Christmas's face from easy shapes cut from wrapping paper.

FATHER CHRISTMAS FACE

What You Need: plain or patterned wrapping paper, scissors, sellotape, cotton wool.

What You Do:

1. It's best to wrap your gift in plain paper. Then, create the cutouts for Father Christmas's features in either patterned wrapping paper, or a different colour of plain paper.

2. Cut out simple shapes to create Father Christmas's features. For example: a large triangle for his cap, two small triangles for his eyes, a small square for his nose, a thin half-circle for his mouth, and another large triangle (turned upside down) for his beard. And two small circles for his rosy cheeks, and a cotton wool ball for the top of Father Christmas's cap.

3. Arrange Father Christmas's face on your parcel.

4. Tape the different shapes onto the parcel.

VI. Invent Your Own Wrapping Paper

GLITTER PAPER

What You Need: old newspapers, wrapping paper, glue, glitter.

What You Do:

1. Wrap your gift as you would normally, but do not add ribbon.

2. Spread out newspapers over your work space and put your gift on top.

3. Lightly apply glue to your gift. (Make sure the glue does not dry before you apply the glitter.) You can write a message, draw a picture, or make a pattern with the glue. Or you can use words to make a pattern. For example, "Ho! Ho! Ho!" can be written all over the paper, in straight lines or at random.
   You can also use glittery words in place of a Christmas tag, or draw a picture and write a message too.

4. Once you have applied the glue, quickly sprinkle the glitter over it. Put on more glitter than you need, so it covers every part of your picture or message.

5. Let the glue and glitter set for a minute or two. Then shake the glitter off onto the newspaper beneath your wrapping paper.

6. Let your pattern dry for another hour before touching it.

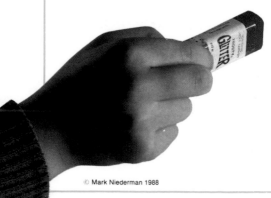

© Mark Niederman 1988

Painting your own wrapping paper with a pretty pattern will make your gift unique.

PAINTBRUSH PAPER

What You Need: newspaper, white drawing paper, sellotape, poster paints or watercolours, a medium-sized or large-sized paintbrush, a small dish of water (to rinse off the brush).

What You Do:

1. Spread newspaper over your work space. Then bring out the rest of your materials.

2. Before you begin to paint, check to make sure the size of your drawing paper will fit your gift. If one sheet is too small, try sellotaping two pieces together.

3. Paint simple patterns on your paper. It's best to stick to patterns, not pictures, so that the pattern will look right when you wrap your gift. (A large picture might end up on the wrong side when you wrap your gift.)

4. Let your painted paper dry before wrapping your gift.

Tony Cenicola

SPONGE PATTERN PAPER

What You Need: newspaper, regular-sized sponge or sponges, plain drawing paper, poster paints, scissors, small dish of water.

Optional: glue and glitter.

What You Do:

1. Spread newspapers over your work space.

2. Check to see if one piece of drawing paper is large enough to cover your gift. If not, sellotape two (or more) pieces together.

3. Dampen a sponge and squeeze the extra water out.

4. With scissors, cut out a simple pattern—like a circle, triangle, or square.

5. Lightly dip one side of the sponge shape into a jar of poster paint.

6. Press the sponge's painted side down onto the paper. Press the sponge down again in another place to make a second print. Keep pressing the sponge down on the paper, making prints. You do not need to dip the sponge back into the paint each time — only when the print gets too light.

7. If you wish to change colours, rinse the sponge shape out in a small dish of water.

8. Let your paper dry completely before wrapping your gift.

Other Suggestions:

a. Use different colours and different sponge shapes for more colourful paper.

b. Apply glue in and around your design and sprinkle glitter over it.

© Ann Hagen Griffiths 1987/Omni-Photo Communications

HOW TO MAKE CHRISTMAS TREE ORNAMENTS

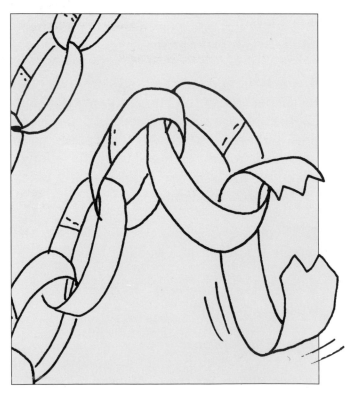

Insert a strip of coloured card through one link and sellotape it together. Keep adding links until your chain is as long as you desire.

Paper Chain

What You Need: coloured card or Christmas wrapping paper, and sellotape.

What You Do:

1. Cut the paper into equal-sized strips, about 2½ centimetres wide and 20 centimetres long (1 inch wide and 8 inches long).

2. Bring the ends of one strip together and hold them together in one hand.

3. Sellotape the ends together with your other hand.

4. Slip another strip through this ring and sellotape those ends together.

5. You can make the chain as long as you want by adding more strips.

Paper Cornucopia (Horn of Plenty)

What You Need: coloured card or sturdy Christmas wrapping paper, sellotape, glue, glitter, and a piece of cotton.

What You Do:

1. Cut out a small rectangular piece of paper, about 13 centimetres wide and 10 centimetres long (5 inches wide and 4 inches long).

2. Decorate one side of the paper (if you're using Christmas paper, decorate the white side), with glitter. Concentrate your efforts on the upper left side of the paper, since that corner will be what shows most.

3. When dry, take the bottom two ends, *right corner over left corner,* and twist the paper until you have a little horn.

4. Punch a tiny hole at the top and insert a piece of cotton.

5. Make a large loop with the thread and tie a knot.

6. Hang your paper cornucopia on the tree.

Felt Ornaments

What You Need: pencil, scissors, pins, squares of felt, sequins, glitter, glue, and cotton.

What You Do:

1. On a piece of felt, draw the pattern outline of your ornament, such as a Christmas tree, angel, bell, or star.

2. Cut the felt around your pattern.

3. Now decorate the felt ornament as you wish. Sew or glue on sequins. Decorate with glitter. Or make a face using other material or other coloured pieces of felt.

4. Cut a tiny hole at the top and insert a piece of cotton.

5. Make a loop with the cotton and tie a knot.

6. Hang your felt ornament on the tree.

Decorated Polystyrene Balls

What You Need: plain polystyrene balls, sequins, dressmaker's pins, ribbon, glitter, glue, scissors, and coloured pipe cleaners.

What You Do:

1. Decorate the balls any way you like. You can attach sequins with dressmaker's pins, or glue on ribbons and glitter. You can make faces or pretty patterns. Use your imagination!

2. When finished, cut a pipe cleaner in half (you may need an adult to help you). Stick it into the ball and bend the top, so it has a hook. Now it's ready to hang.

Bead Rings

What You Need: brightly coloured beads, needle, cotton, and scissors.

What You Do:

1. Thread your needle with an approximately 15-centimetre-long (6-inch-long) piece of cotton. (Make sure the needle fits through the holes in your beads.)

2. Bring the two ends together and tie a knot, about 2½ centimetres (an inch) from the end.

3. Now string your beads on the cotton, stopping when there is only 4 centimetres (1½ inches) of cotton left at the top.

4. Form the bead chain into a circle and tie the two ends together in a knot.

5. Cut the needle and any loose cotton free, and your ornament is ready to hang on the tree.

Baby-in-a-Cradle Ornaments

What You Need: half a walnut shell, cotton wool ball, small pearl button, thin-tipped paint brush, acrylic or poster paint, glue, a small piece of material (about 2½ centimetres or 1 inch), string or slender ribbon, scissors, and sellotape.

What You Do:

1. Take half a walnut shell and put a cotton wool ball in it.

2. With a small paintbrush, paint two eyes and a small dot for a mouth on a small button.

3. When dry, glue the back of the button to the small piece of material, which will be a "blanket."

4. When dry, gently lift the blanket and button and place on top of the cotton wool ball.

5. Take a string or ribbon (about 25 centimetres [10 inches] long) and double it over. Tape the centre of the ribbon to the bottom of the walnut.

6. Tie the string or ribbon in a large loop that extends well over the top of the walnut. Snip unnecessary ends, and hang your baby-in-a-cradle on the tree.

Tin Ornament

What You Need: a clean throwaway aluminium pan or a sheet of aluminium from the crafts shop (tin foil is too soft); thick felt tip pens; varnish; or clear nail varnish; string.

What You Do:

1. First draw your pattern on the aluminium sheet.

2. Cover your work space with newspaper, and place the aluminium sheet on top.

3. Cut out the pattern on the aluminium.

4. Colour it with felt tip pens.

5. To finish, use varnish or clear nail varnish to coat the surface.

6. Make a small hole at top (with pen point or the tip of a knitting needle).

7. Loop bright string or cotton through hole and secure with knot. Now it's ready to hang.

Use felt tips to decorate a shiny tin ornament.

Christmas Tree Bulbs

What You Need: clear glass Christmas tree bulbs (ball-shaped glass ornaments); your favourite small Christmas accessories or toys; and ribbons, cotton wool, sequins, glitter, and glue.

What You Do:

1. Remove the top (hook part) from the bulb.

2. Fill the bulb with such things as: cotton wool balls, a sprig of holly or mistletoe, a small toy, or bright strands of ribbon. You can also add a small picture. Simply roll it up and stick it through the top—it will unfold inside.

3. If you wish, decorate the outside of the bulb—though be sure not to cover up what you put inside. Lightly coat part of the bulb with glue, then sprinkle on some glitter. Or glue a ribbon around the centre. Let the bulb dry.

4. When finished, put the top back on. Then hang on the tree.

Note: It's also nice to put a personal touch on other types of ornaments. There's often room for painting a message, such as your name or "Merry Christmas," and the year.

If the ornament is a gift, paint the name of the person to whom you are giving it, and any other message you wish.

© B. Taylor 1987/FPG Intl.

HOW TO MAKE CHRISTMAS DECORATIONS FOR YOUR HOME

A Christmas tree in the living room and yummy aromas coming from the kitchen help set the holiday mood in any home. But you can create even more seasonal spirit by adding decorative touches of your own. The following pages show a variety of fun ways to do this.

GLUING TIPS

White Glue that comes in a plastic bottle is good for almost every project listed in this book. It is easy to handle and sticks well to most objects.

White glue is good for working with glitter. Use your little finger like a pen or pencil, to write or draw with the glue. Then simply sprinkle on the glitter.

Rubber Cement is better to use than white glue when working with paper. White glue sticks fast and hard when two pieces of paper are glued together. For that reason, the paper is hard to pull apart, if you have made a mistake, and you will almost always have to

start over again. Also, if white glue comes out around the edges, it will leave a mark; rubber cement can be gently rubbed off when dry and will not leave a mark.

Rubber cement is also good for gluing other things onto paper. If you make a mistake, it's possible to gently pull the item off the paper, gently rub the rubber cement off both pieces, and start over again—your mistake will hardly show.

Rubber cement also sticks better than regular white glue, when gluing two pieces of felt together.

Rubber cement, which usually comes with a brush attached to the bottle cap, is easy to apply to large surfaces. However, the big brush makes it hard to apply to small items, such as narrow ribbons and sequins. The brush also makes rubber cement less effective than glue when working with glitter.

When working with either type of glue, remember not to apply too much of it. Too much glue makes a decoration look sloppy, especially when it comes out around the edges. You can always add more glue later.

Christmas Table Centrepieces—A festive touch to a holiday table.

What You Need: sturdy paper, scissors, pencil, dressmaker's pins, felt.

Optional: sequins, string, ribbon, different coloured felt, and glue.

What You Do:

1. On a large piece of paper (20 centimetres x 25 centimetres [8 inches x 10 inches]), draw a simple object or figure, such as a Christmas tree, star, angel, or candle.

2. Cut the drawing out and place it on a large piece of felt.

3. Pin the drawing to the felt and cut around the pattern.

4. Decorate the felt Christmas shape as you like. You can glue on sequins, decorate the edges with string or ribbon, and add smaller cut-out shapes of felt.

Christmas Stockings

Your own personally decorated stocking to hang up on the mantelpiece.

(This makes a fine decoration, but it is not sturdy enough for Father Christmas to fill.)

What You Need: a piece of red felt twice as big as your stocking will be, heavy paper, dressmaker's pins, pencil, string, other pieces of different coloured felt or fabric, and glue.

What You Do:

1. Draw a pattern for the stocking on a heavy piece of paper.

2. Cut the stocking pattern out.

3. Fold the red felt in half (or place two equal-sized pieces together).

4. Pin the paper stocking pattern to the felt.

5. Cut carefully around the pattern. When you finish, you should have two stocking-shaped pieces of felt.

6. Decorate the felt stocking pieces. Make sure you only decorate the outside portion of each piece. With the other coloured pieces of felt or fabric, you can cut out letters to make your name, or simple Christmas objects like a star, ornament, Christmas tree or gift. If you know how to sew, use a needle and cotton to attach sequins. Decorate with colourful string, which you can glue on.

7. After decorating the outer side of each stocking piece, glue the two sides together. Put the glue along only the outside edge of the undecorated side of one of the stockings. Make sure not to glue the top edges together. Press the two pieces together. For extra strength, sew the two sides together carefully.

8. To hang, snip a small hole in the upper right hand corner of each side of the stocking. Pull a piece of string through, and tie it in a loop.

© Mark Niederman 1988

"Klockastrang" or "Bell Pull"

A festive door decoration that announces visitors' arrival with the jingle of bells when the door is opened.

This decoration can be as large as you like, but beginners may want to start with something small. A good size would be 25 centimetres wide x 30 centimetres long (10 inches wide x 12 inches long).

What You Need: a piece of green, white, or red felt, measuring 25 centimetres x 30 centimetres (10 inches x 12 inches), scissors, dressmaker's pins, wool, smaller pieces of coloured felt or other fabric, ribbon, glue, small "jingle bells," needle and cotton.

What You Do:

1. Decorate the Klockastrang in the same ways suggested for the Christmas stocking. You may also want to glue ribbon strands down the front. Sew the jingle bells along the edges.

2. To make a handle, cut a small hole out in the top centre. Pull a piece of wool through and tie it in a loop.

Hang a klockastrang on the door to hear a jingle each time it opens or closes.

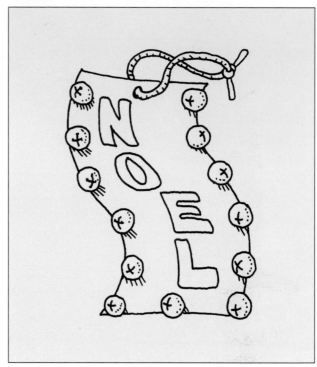

Christmas Place Cards

What You Need: last year's Christmas cards, table place cards, and glue or sellotape.

What You Do:

1. Cut out an object (an ornament, Christmas tree, candle) or a figure (Baby Jesus, Father Christmas, or animal) from the old Christmas cards.

2. Put glue or sellotape onto the back of the cut-out, where it will stick to the place card.

3. Stick the cut-out onto the place card.

© Mark Niederman · 988

Snowball Tree

What You Need: polystyrene cone (available in crafts shops), green card, cotton wool balls, toothpicks or dressmaker's pins, glue (and possibly, sellotape), and glitter.

What You Do:

1. Take a polystyrene cone and wrap it in the card. To do this, fold the card around the cone, tucking the upper right hand corner of the card around the point of the cone. Bring the rest of the card around the cone and sellotape the two sides together.

If your card does not completely cover the cone, patch the space with a small square of green card. Stick the patch over the space with sellotape or glue.

2. Stick the cotton wool balls onto the cone with dressmaker's pins or toothpicks.

3. Lightly dab some glue onto the edge of the cotton wool balls.

4. Sprinkle glitter over the glue.

5. Let your "tree" dry completely before moving it.

Place your picture right-side-up on the sticky side of the clear sticky back paper.

Then place the sticky side of the second *piece of sticky back paper down on top of the picture.*

Holiday Table Mat

This table mat (or place mat) wipes off easily and can be used over and over. Make the mat any size you like. Take a ruler and measure a table mat at home. The size suggested in these directions, 43 centimetres wide x 29 centimetres high (17 inches wide x 11½ inches high), will allow some of the picture to show, even when covered with a plate.

The clear sticky back plastic called for is available at most hardware shops.

What You Need: a piece of drawing paper in the size suggested above, clear sticky back plastic (enough to cover *both* sides of your paper), a ruler, coloured felt tip pens, coloured card, sequins, glitter, and glue.

What You Do:

1. On the paper, draw a picture with Christmas as the theme. You could also use coloured card to cut out and paste on small objects, such as Christmas trees and Snowflakes.

2. Glue on some sequins and glitter, if you like.

3. With a ruler, measure the size of your picture. Let's say your picture is the suggested size, 43 centimetres wide x 29 centimetres high (17 inches wide x 11½ inches high).

4. Spread out your sticky back plastic. With your ruler, measure and cut out a piece 44 centimetres wide x 30 centimetres high (17½ inches wide x 12 inches high). (It's good to have a little extra around the edges.)

5. Measure and cut out another piece of sticky back plastic, the same size as the first.

6. Before applying the sticky back plastic, make sure your picture is clean and that any paint or glue has dried. Peel the sticky back plastic off its backing sheet and lay it on your work space so the sticky side is facing up.

7. You may want to ask an adult to help you place the back side of your picture on top of the sticky back plastic, as straight and evenly as possible.

8. Peel backing off your second piece of sticky back plastic. Lay the sticky back plastic on your work space, sticky side up.

9. Place the front of your picture down on the sticky side of the second piece of sticky back plastic. Try to match the sides and corners as well as possible.

10. Trim any edges of the sticky back plastic that don't match.

Many beautiful designs can be created by making cuts in a piece of folded paper.

© Mark Niederman 1988

Snowflakes

What You Need: paper (plain or coloured), scissors.

Optional: pretty thread or wool.

What You Do:

1. Cut a circle from a piece of paper.

2. Fold it in half.

3. Fold it in half again.

4. Cut out shapes along the folds.

Optional:

1. For a Christmas tree ornament, punch a small hole at the top and put a piece of thread or wool through it. Tie the string to make a loop and hang your snowflake on the tree.

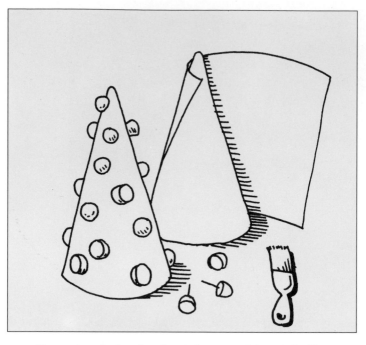

Wrap a piece of coloured card around a cone and decorate it with fruit gums.

Sugarplum Tree

What You Need: a polystyrene cone, scissors, sellotape or glue, coloured card, glitter, toothpicks, fruit gums, marshmallows.

What You Do:

1. Wrap the polystyrene cone in the card. To do this, fold the card around the cone, tucking the upper right corner around the point of the cone.

2. Bring the rest of the card around the cone and sellotape the two sides together. If your card does not completely cover the cone, patch the space with a small square of green card. Stick the patch over the space with sellotape or glue.

3. Lightly brush on glue.

4. Sprinkle glitter over the cone.

5. Place a fruit gum and a small marshmallow on a toothpick and stick it onto the cone. Keep adding these until the cone tree is full.

Pomander Ball

A nice and easy decoration that also adds the scent of Christmas to your house. Try hanging it in your wardrobe or bathroom, or the entrance to your house.

What You Need: an apple or orange, box of whole cloves, small bag, 1 tablespoon cinnamon, 1 tablespoon orris root (available at most chemists), and string or ribbon.

Optional: tissue paper.

What You Do:

1. Take a whole, unpeeled apple or orange and stick the cloves into the fruit. (The cloves absorb the fruit juices, so the fruit won't rot.)

2. Keep sticking in cloves, until the whole fruit is covered.

3. Fill a small bag with 1 tablespoon of cinnamon and 1 tablespoon of powdered orris root and shake the clove-covered fruit in it.

© Mark Niederman 1988

Optional:

4. Wrap your pomander ball in pretty tissue paper.

5. Tie a pretty ribbon or bright string around the ball.

Picture Pencil Holder

What You Need: an empty, clean tin, coloured card, or plain-coloured wrapping paper or sticky back plastic, sellotape, scissors, paper doily, string, glue, and a small close-up photograph or drawing of yourself.

What You Do:

1. Wrap the tin in coloured card, wrapping paper, or sticky back plastic. To do this, hold one end of a piece of your paper next to the tin and wrap the other end around it.

2. Sellotape the two sides of paper together (not necessary for sticky back plastic). If there is extra paper up top, simply push it down inside the tin. Smooth the extra paper until it lies flat against the tin.

3. Cut the picture of yourself into an oval shape.

4. Cut the paper doily into an oval shape, slightly bigger than your picture.

5. Stick your picture onto the oval doily. Let it dry.

6. Stick the doily/picture onto the tin.

7. Add colourful wool or string around the top and bottom.

Pretty Things to Do with Tree Branches and Pine Cones

These ideas are simple yet lovely ways to make use of leftover Christmas tree branches, as well as bare branches and pine cones that have fallen off trees.

GOLD BRANCHES

What You Need: evergreen branch, clean sponge, newspaper, paintbrush, gold paint, and a vase.

What You Do:

1. Spread out newspaper over your work space.

2. Take an evergreen branch and cut off its lower leaves or needles.

3. Wipe the other needles clean with a damp sponge and let them dry.

4. Paint the whole branch, or just the tips—whichever you like.

5. Fill a vase with water, and put the bare ends in it.

FRUIT GUM BRANCHES

What You Need: prickly, thorny branches; fruit gums; and a vase.

What You Do:

1. Wash and dry the branches. Be careful not to prick yourself.

2. Stick a small fruit gum on each thorn.

3. Put in a vase with *no* water.

GLITTER BRANCHES

For these branches, you can use either regular white glue or a paste made from flour and water that you put on with a paintbrush.

The flour-and-water paste creates a kind of "snow" effect and also glues on the glitter. Though it doesn't go on as smoothly as white glue, it's white colour will last.

To make the paste, mix 1 tablespoon flour and 2 teaspoons water in a small dish or cup.

White glue goes on smoothly and holds the glitter well. However, its white colour soon disappears and will no longer look like snow.

What You Need: a bare branch with small twigs on it, a small paintbrush, newspaper, flour-and-water paste (described above).

What You Do:

1. Spread out newspaper over your work space.

2. Paint part of the branch with the flour-and-water paste (or white glue).

3. Shake glitter over the branch.

4. Let the branches dry.

5. Put in a vase with *no* water.

DECORATED PINE CONES

What You Need: newspaper, glue (or the flour-and-water paste described in Glitter Branches), pine cones, white paint, paintbrush, sequins, tweezers, glitter, and silver or gold string.

What You Do:

1. Spread newspaper over your work space.

2. To give the appearance of "snow," paint the pine cone edges white. Let the paint dry.

3. Weave gold or silver thread around the pine cone petals, from top to bottom.

© Mark Niederman 1988

4. Squeeze glue over the pine cone petals—do not let dry.

5. Sprinkle glitter over the glue.

6. Glue on sequins. For placing sequins in difficult places, use a pair of tweezers.

CHRISTMAS CRACKERS

These crackers open with a pleasing "pop!" to reveal a tiny treat inside.

What You Need: tubes from the inside of lavatory rolls, wrapping foil or crepe paper or tissue in Christmas colours, glue, and an assortment of tiny gifts, such as small sweets, rubbers, or pencil sharpeners.

What You Do:

1. Place a tiny gift inside each tube.

2. Then cut squares of foil, crepe paper, or tissue about 10 centimetres (4 inches) longer than the tubes.

3. Place each filled tube at the centre of one end of each square of foil, and roll the tube up.

4. Use a spot of glue to hold the foil in place.

5. Let the glue dry, then twist both ends of the foil to seal the ends of the tube and keep the gift inside.

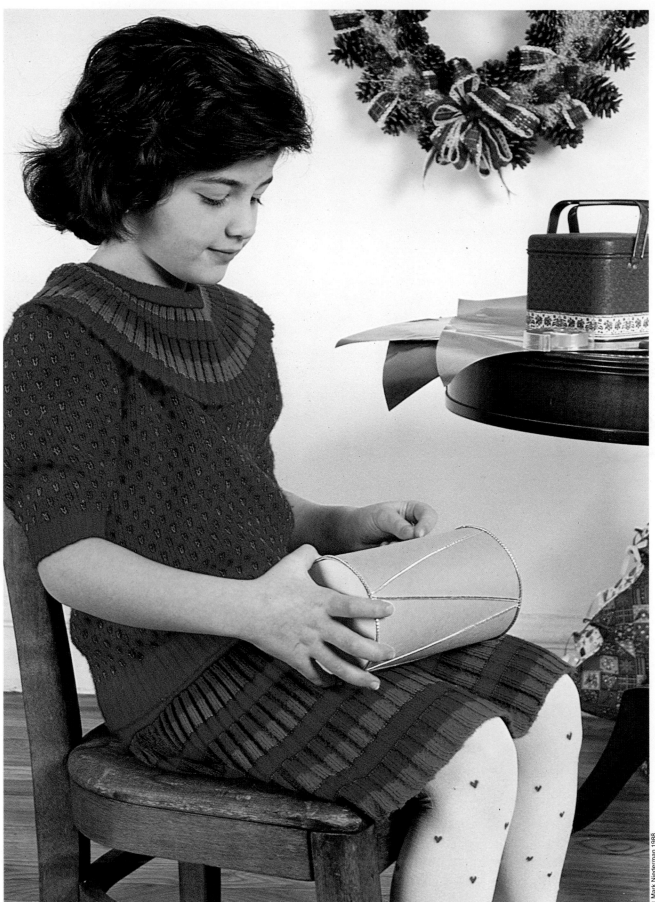

The Drummer Boy's Drum

What You Need: a large empty dishwashing liquid bottle; wrapping paper, coloured card or sticky back plastic; stiff card; wool; sellotape; glue; scissors; compass.

What You Do:

1. Cut the bottle in half. Keep the base half.

2. Cut a piece of wrapping paper, coloured card, or sticky back plastic large enough to fit around your bottle base.

3. Hold one side of the coloured card against the bottle, and bring the other side of the card around. Sellotape the two sides together.

4. If your card goes over the top of the bottle base, simply push the card down and flatten it against the inside of the bottle.

5. Make the bottle lid by drawing around the bottle base on the stiff card. Use a compass to draw another circle outside the bottle base circle. (It should have a diametre of about four centimetres more than the bottle base circle.)

6. Cut out the bigger circle. Then carefully cut lots of little triangles out of the two centimetre lip around the bottle base circle. Fold each remaining piece of lip down at right angles to the base circle. Sellotape in place.

7. Place the unwrapped lid on the bottle. (The drum sounds better with an unwrapped lid.)

Optional:

8. Decorate the drum by gluing on yarn or ribbon.

Balloon Ball

All your friends will want to know how you made this interesting decoration.

What You Need: a balloon (not *too* big, until you know how to make them); several metres of thick green, red, and white string; a dish of glue or liquid starch; a large bowl; cotton wool balls; sprig of mistletoe or holly, or a lightweight Christmas ornament.

What You Do:

1. Blow up a small balloon and tie the end in a knot.

2. Dip the strings, one at a time, in the glue or liquid starch and coil the wet strings around the balloon so that the whole balloon is covered.

3. Set the stringy, wet balloon in a large bowl and let it dry. This may take several days.

4. When the strings are dry, pop the balloon.

5. Carefully remove the balloon pieces. What's left is a coiled string ornament.

6. You can tie a string through it and hang it from your ceiling.

7. Before hanging, cut a small hole in the bottom.

8. Put a fluffy layer of cotton wool inside and add a sprig of mistletoe, holly, or a lightweight Christmas ornament.

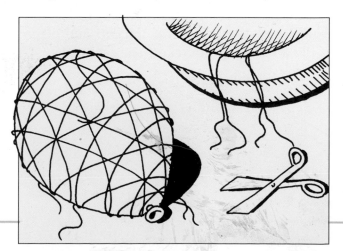

Christmas Countdown Chain

What You Need: scissors, coloured card or wrapping paper.

What You Do:

1. Make a holiday paper chain (see directions on page 74), 25 links long, and number each link from 1 to 25.

2. Beginning December 1, take off one link each day, starting with the link numbered 25. (Or make the chain 50 links long and take off two links every day.)

3. Watch the chain grow shorter and shorter, as Christmas Day grows closer and closer.

Holiday Party Hats

What You Need: tissue paper, pinking shears, glue, and coloured pencils.

What You Do:

1. Cut a wide strip of tissue paper long enough to wrap around your head.

2. Cut one edge into a zig-zag shape or another decorative shape with the pinking shears or with ordinary scissors. Decorate your crown with coloured pencils, if you like.

3. Next, glue the two short ends together to form a crown.

4. Let the glue dry completely, and the crown is ready to wear or fold up and place inside a Christmas cracker (see page 87).

© David White/Stockfile

How to Make an Advent Calendar

Advent calendars are a German custom that has been carried over to Great Britain and North America. An Advent calendar is a special way of marking the days from December 1 until Christmas Eve or Christmas Day.

Most Advent calendars are large Christmas pictures with twenty-four or twenty-five little windows cut into them. Before December 1, all the windows are closed, so that the outside of each one blends into the picture. But starting December 1, a window is opened each day until Christmas.

Each window is numbered, so that you know which window to open on what day. (For example, on December 5, you open Window 5.) Behind each window is a different picture, and it's always a surprise to see what the picture is.

Here's how to make your own:

What You Need: drawing paper, coloured pencils or felt tip pens, scissors, sellotape or glue, and glitter.

What You Do:

1. Using a pencil, draw a Christmas scene on a large piece of paper. The scene can be anything you like—your home or town, an imaginary Christmas tree forest with fairies and elves, Father Christmas up at his North Pole workshop, or the Nativity scene, with Mary, Joseph, the shepherds, and three wise men looking at the Baby Jesus in the manger.

Instead of a Christmas scene, you can also draw a large figure like a Father Christmas, a Christmas tree, or even a giant gingerbread man.

2. Once you have a picture you like, lightly pencil in twenty-four or twenty-five little windows. The windows can be any size that best fits your page. Remember, though, that if you make a tiny window, the picture behind it will have to be tiny also.

To make a medium-sized window, draw three sides of a box: a 2½-centimetre (1-inch) line going sideways, a 2-centimetre (¾-inch) line going lengthwise, and another 2½-centimetre (1-inch) line going sideways.

Make the 2-centimetre (¾-inch) line on the right-hand side, so the window will open from right to left.

3. Number the windows.

4. Go over your drawing in felt tip pen or coloured pencil. (Be careful not to lose your window lines.)

5. Cut the three sides to your windows. This part can be tricky; do it slowly, or ask an adult to help you, so you do not tear your drawing. Once that part is done, the outside of your Advent calendar is complete.

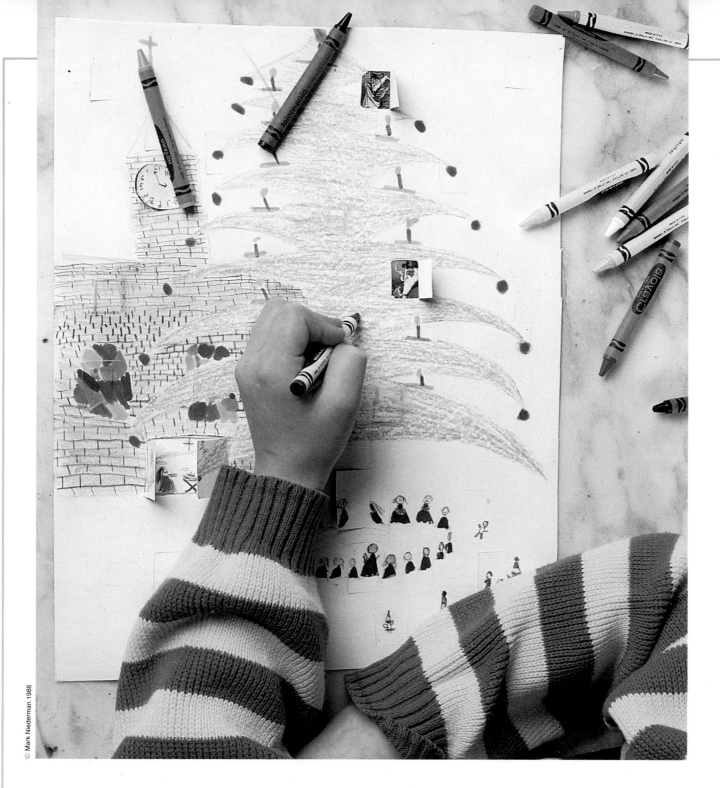

6. For the little pictures behind the windows, take out one or two clean sheets of drawing paper. Use this paper to make twenty-four or twenty-five drawings that will fit behind the squares on your Christmas picture. Make the space between each drawing at least as big as the window box.

The drawings can be related to your picture or simply drawings of Christmas or the whole holiday season. Other suggestions might include a picture (or the name) of a friend, grandparent, pet, or anyone special in your life.

7. Cut around each picture with enough extra space to cover the back of the window.

8. Sellotape or lightly glue the border of each drawing to the back side of the calendar, over a window square. The picture should be facing down; that way, when the window is opened from the front, the picture will show there.

9. Your Advent calendar is finished! But if you wish, decorate your picture and the windows with a little glitter.

How to Cook Christmas Treats

Before You Start to Cook

- Ask an adult if it is alright to use the kitchen.
- Be sure to wash your hands.
- Read the recipe carefully to make sure you understand it.
- Check the list of ingredients your recipe calls for—do you have them all?
- Check to see that you have all the cooking tools (chopping board, the right size pan, etc.) your recipe calls for.
- Put on an apron to keep your clothes clean.

While You Are Cooking

- Ask an adult before you use a sharp knife, tin opener, electric mixer, cooker, or oven.
- Use oven gloves to protect your hands when handling any dish that has been on the cooker or in the oven.
- When cooking, keep the handles of pots and pans turned toward the side of the cooker to avoid knocking into them and causing spills.

- Use a chopping board when slicing or chopping ingredients. Do not cut anything on the worktop, unless you have permission from an adult to do so.
- Be sure to ask for help, when...
   —you need to pour batter from a large, heavy bowl into a pan;
   —you need to pour liquid from a large, heavy bottle or container;
   —you are unsure about a certain measurement or ingredient.

When You Finish Cooking

Try to make the kitchen look as clean as, (or cleaner than!) when you began. To do this:

- Wash all the dishes, pans, and tools you used.
- Take a sponge and wipe the worktop clean. You may also need to wipe around the cooker and on the oven and refrigerator doors.
- Put away all remaining ingredients.

John Pemberton

© Mark Niederman 1988

Cooking Tools You May Need

FOR PREPARATION:

Knife
Chopping board
Wooden spoon
Rubber spatula or scraper
Metal or non-stick spatula
Bowls: large, medium, and small
Saucepans: medium and small
Blender
Electric mixer
Rolling pin

FOR MEASURING:

Measuring spoon: 1, 2, 5 ml (¼, ½, 1 tsp)
  measures
Kitchen scales for dry ingredients
Measuring jug for liquid ingredients

FOR BAKING:

Bread tin
33cm x 23cm (13 in x 9 in) rectangular pan
20cm (8 in) square pan
20cm (8 in) round cake pan
33cm x 23cm (13 in x 9 in) baking tray

Measuring Hints

• Use a measuring jug for liquids when a recipe calls for 55ml (2 fl oz) or more of milk, water, juice, or vegetable oil. Put the cup down on a worktop or table and pour the liquid until it reaches the proper mark on the measuring jug. Look at the mark at eye level to make sure it is right.

• Use kitchen scales for dry ingredients such as sugar (white, brown, castor, and icing), flour, and any other type of dry substance, when the recipe calls for 25g (1 oz) or more. When the recipe calls for less than 25g (1 oz) of something, use measuring spoons.

• When measuring salt, pour gently from the container while standing over the sink or rubbish bin. If you don't have a salt container, shake a good amount of salt from a salt cellar into a cup and dip your measuring spoon into that.

• When measuring baking soda, baking powder, cornflour, or spices, dip the measuring spoon into the tin. Then level the top off with a butter knife.

• When measuring butter, leave the butter out of the refrigerator until it is soft enough to be scooped into a spoon.

• If you want to make twice as much food as a recipe in this book will make, you will have to double the amount of each ingredient. For example, if the recipe calls for one egg, use two.

   When you want to make only half as much food as a recipe will make, use half the amount of each ingredient the recipe calls for. For example, if it calls for 5ml (1 tsp) use only 2½ml (½ tsp).

   If a recipe calls for 1 egg, and you need to divide it in half, crack the egg in a separate bowl and beat it with a fork. When the yolk and white are mixed well, you can pour half into your recipe.

John Pemberton

A Child's Glossary of Cooking Tips, Terms, and Ingredients

Bake—to cook in an oven.

Beat—to mix rapidly, stirring many times with a spoon or an electric beater.

Blend—to combine two or more ingredients thoroughly.

Brown Sugar—There are two main types of brown sugar, light and dark. These sugars are moister than white or "granulated" sugar. They also have a stronger flavour, especially dark brown sugar.

Brown sugar is lumpy and must be measured in a certain way. To do it properly, spoon the sugar into the pan of a set of kitchen scales, breaking up the lumps as you do so.

Brown sugar should be stored in a tightly closed plastic bag in the refrigerator, as it tends to dry out and harden easily.

Butter—Real butter is a product made from milk or cream. Margarine, which is similar to butter, is made mostly from vegetable oils. In this book, when a recipe calls for "butter," you can substitute margarine instead.

Chop—to cut into little pieces with a knife, blender, or food processor. Make sure you have an adult's permission before you chop. Also be sure an adult is with you when you use a food processor or blender.

Flour—Some recipes will call for you to **grease and flour a baking tin.** To do this, rub the bottom and sides of the tin with butter or margarine (see "Grease" below), and drop about a tablespoon of flour into the tin. Holding the tin over the sink, shake it until the flour is spread evenly around the tin. It helps to hold the tin in one hand and use the other hand to gently tap the tin.

To flour a rolling pin, take a little butter or vegetable oil and rub it on the rolling pin. Then sprinkle a little flour on the pin with your hand. The flour should prevent your dough from sticking to the pin.

Granulated sugar or **white sugar**—This is the most common type of sugar. It is smooth, like sand, and pours easily without having to be firmly packed down by hand.

Grease—Some recipes will call for you to **grease a baking tin**: take a slice of butter and use a piece of grease-proof paper to spread it evenly over the sides and bottom of the pan. Greasing helps prevent food from sticking to the pan.

Icing Sugar—This sugar resembles flour and is most often used in making frostings. If you don't have any, buy some! Ordinary white or brown sugar won't work as a substitute.

Measures (Level, Heaped, and Rounded spoonfuls)—Some of the recipes call for level, heaped, or rounded measurements in their directions:

Level—To measure a level spoonful of a recipe ingredient, scoop up some of the ingredient in the appropriate measure, and level it off (make it even with the top edges of the spoon) with a butter knife or another spoon. All recipes call for level measures unless they say otherwise.

Heaped—This means the measurement does not have to be precise. Scoop up the ingredient in the appropriate sized spoon but DON'T level it off.

Rounded—Biscuits are often dropped by "rounded teaspoonfuls" onto a baking sheet. To do this, dip a teaspoon into the dough. Then, using your fingers or another spoon, push the biscuit dough from the teaspoon onto the baking sheet. Place each small ball of dough about 2½cm (1 in) or more away from the last one, if the recipe calls for it. Biscuit dough spreads out as it bakes; placing the dough balls far apart will prevent them from spreading out to become one big biscuit!

Melt—heat a substance (like butter) in a pot or pan until it becomes liquid.

Non-stick sauce pans—These kinds of sauce pans, available at most hardware or department stores, usually do not need to be floured or greased to prevent sticking. Even so, it's not a bad idea to lightly grease your pan, anyway.

Separating An Egg — Sometimes a recipe calls for just an egg yolk or just an egg white. It is then necessary to separate the two different parts. To do this:

1. Take out two small bowls.
2. Gently crack the eggshell on the side of one bowl as evenly as possible, so that you get two equal halves. One half of the egg shell should contain all egg white. The other half should contain the egg yolk, plus some more egg white.

3. Let the egg white from the first half drip into one of the bowls. Keep the other half of the eggshell upright. It is important not to let any yolk mix in with the white.

4. When the eggshell with the egg white is empty, transfer the egg yolk to that shell half. In doing so, try to let some of the extra egg white from the second shell drip into the egg white bowl.

5. Keep shifting the egg yolk from one eggshell half to the other, until all the extra egg white is in the first bowl. Then very gently slip the egg yolk from the shell and into the second bowl.

Sift—This usually refers to putting flour through a sifter, or sieve, which makes the flour smoother. It is possible to buy pre-sifted flour; it will say "pre-sifted" on the package. If you don't have a sifter, stir the flour with a fork to remove any lumps.

Lynn Karlin 1987

Christmas Party Cones

1 regular-sized box any flavour cake mix
Any ingredients the cake mix calls for
24 flat-bottomed ice-cream cones
Icing (any flavour)

1. Heat oven to Gas Mark 4/180° C/350° F, and have ready baking sheets or tins large enough to hold 24 ice-cream cones.

2. Prepare the cake mix in a medium-sized mixing bowl. Follow the directions on the box, but do not pour the batter into a pan or bake it.

3. Fill the ice-cream cones with cake batter. To do this, hold each ice-cream cone in one hand over the bowl. Spoon cake batter into the cone until it is half full. Place the filled cones on baking sheets or in the cups of the tartlet tin.

4. Bake for 30 minutes. Let cool before icing. (For icing recipe, see page 103.)

Makes 24 cones.

Easy Egg Nog

This traditional Christmas drink tastes like a vanilla milkshake.
1l (35 fl oz) milk
4 eggs
2 tsp vanilla extract
85g (3 oz) sugar
450ml (16 fl oz) vanilla ice-cream
Nutmeg

1. Pour all the ingredients into a blender.

2. Cover and blend for 1 minute.

3. Pour into 4 glasses and sprinkle each glass with a dash of nutmeg.

Christmas Pudding

Remember to start this traditional treat at least one month before Christmas.

110g (4 oz) brown sugar
170g (6 oz) black raisins
170g (6 oz) golden raisins
170g (6 oz) currants
170g (6 oz) mixed candied orange peel, lemon peel, citron, and cherries
85g (3 oz) beef suet, ground
2 large eggs

85ml (3 fl oz) brandy
55g (2 oz) plain flour
½ tsp salt
½ tsp ground nutmeg
½ tsp cinnamon
Pinch mace
Brandy Butter (recipe rollows)

1. Combine the sugar, raisins, currants, candied fruit, and ground suet in a large bowl and mix well with a wooden spoon.

2. Next, stir in the eggs and 35ml (1 fl oz) of the brandy and blend well.

3. Then, mix in the flour, salt, nutmeg, cinnamon, and mace.

4. Carefully pour the pudding mixture into a 1-l basin (1¾ pint) or pudding mould (you may want to ask an adult for help). Tightly cover the top with foil.

5. Place a wire rack or stand in the bottom of a large stock pot, and add water to just below the level of the rack or stand. Place the pudding basin on top of the rack, making sure the basin is above the water, and not in it. Bring the water to a boil.

6. Boil the pudding for 4 to 5 hours, adding water to keep the level constant.

7. Remove the pudding from the pot of water and allow it to cool completely. Make sure the foil cover is on tightly, and store the pudding in a cool place for 1 month.

8. To reheat the pudding, repeat step 5, steaming the pudding for only 1 hour.

Serves 8.

Brandy Butter

55g (2 oz) unsalted butter, softened
110g (4 oz) castor sugar
55ml (2 fl oz) brandy

Mix the butter and sugar together with an electric mixer or wooden spoon until creamy. Add the brandy a bit at a time, and mix well unti the sauce is fluffy.

Makes 170g (6 oz).

Chocolate Butter Icing

85g (3 oz) butter
55g (2 oz) unsweetened powdered cocoa
55ml (2 fl oz) hot water
⅛ tsp salt
225g (8 oz) icing sugar
1 tsp vanilla extract

1. Melt the butter in a medium-sized saucepan on the cooker, over low heat.

2. Add and blend in the cocoa.

3. Remove the saucepan from the heat and add the water and salt.

4. Stir and slowly add the sugar and vanilla. Cool before using.
Makes enough icing for 6 cupcakes.

Mince Pies

1 apple, peeled, cored and finely chopped
2 heaped tablespoons mincemeat
1 (225g [8 oz]) packet frozen puff pastry
Flour, Milk, Icing sugar

1. Heat the oven to Gas Mark 6/200° C/400° F.

2. In a small bowl, stir together the apple and mincemeat and mix well.

3. Unfold the pastry on a clean work surface that has been sprinkled with a bit of flour. With a rolling pin, roll the pastry out thinly. Then, let it rest for 10 minutes.

4. After the dough has rested, use a round cutter to make 24 circles of pastry as close together as possible. You can reroll the trimmings if you need to in order to make 24 circles.

5. Line 12 tartlet tins with half of the pastry circles.

6. Spoon 1 teaspoon mincemeat in the middle of each circle.

7. Dip your finger into a little water and dampen the edges of the remaining pastry circles. Place these circles on top of the ones in the tins, and press the edges together to seal them.

8. Make 2 or 3 tiny slits in the top of each pie.

9. Brush each pie with a little milk and place the tins in the oven. Bake for 20 minutes until golden brown.

10. Sprinkle the tops with icing sugar and serve.
Makes 12 pies.

Mincemeat

100g (3½ oz) candied peel, minced
675g (1½ lb) stoned raisins, minced
450g (1 lb) cooking apples, peeled, cored, and chopped
350g (12½ oz) currants
225g (8 oz) sultanas
175g (6 oz) shredded suet
½ level tsp mixed spice
2 lemons
450g (1 lb) soft brown sugar
5 tablespoons rum, brandy, or sherry

Place the first seven ingredients in a large bowl, and mix well. Grate the rind and squeeze the juice from the lemons and add to the bowl along with the sugar and rum, brandy, or sherry, and mix very well. Let the bowl stand overnight, covered with a cloth. Then spoon the mincemeat into pastry tartlets and bake.

Makes 2½ kg of mincemeat.

Holiday Popcorn

There are several ways to make popcorn—with a popcorn machine, with a microwave, with prepackaged kernels in a container shaken over the cooker, or by the traditional method. Choose the way that's easiest for you. Ask an adult to help you if you have never made popcorn before.

675g (1½ lb) popcorn
85g (3 oz) butter
25g (1 oz) sugar
¼ tsp cinnamon
⅛ tsp nutmeg

1. Put the cooked popcorn in an extra large bowl. Set the bowl aside.

2. Melt the butter in a small saucepan on the cooker, over low heat. Turn the handle to one side.

3. Pour the butter over the popcorn and lightly toss it with 2 spoons so that the popcorn is coated with the butter.

4. Combine the sugar, cinnamon, and nutmeg in a small- to medium-sized bowl.

5. Sprinkle the sugar mixture over the popcorn. Toss the popcorn to coat it completely.

Makes about 3 cups popcorn.

HOLIDAY CRAFTS AND RECIPES 105

Traditional Christmas Cake

55g (2 oz) blanched almonds, chopped
1 lemon, juice reserved, and rind, grated
340g (12 oz) raisins
340g (12 oz) currants
340g (12 oz) sultanas
55g (2 oz) cut and mixed peel
85g (3 oz) glace cherries
225g (8 oz) flour
⅛ tsp salt
1½ tsp mixed spice
225g (8 oz) butter
225g (8 oz) brown sugar
4 eggs
25ml (1 fl oz) black treacle
55ml (2 fl oz) brandy

1.   Heat the oven to Gas Mark 2/150°C/300°F.

2.   Grease a round cake tin, measuring 20cm (8 in) across, and line it with two layers of greaseproof paper. Then grease the paper as well.

3.   In a large mixing bowl, combine the almonds, lemon rind, raisins, currants, sultanas, mixed peel, and glace cherries. Set aside.

4.   Then, sift the flour onto a large plate, and mix in the salt and spice.

5.   In another large bowl, cream the butter and sugar together until light and fluffy.

6.   Crack one of the eggs into the bowl, add 25g (1 oz) of the flour mixture, and beat the egg in. Repeat with the remaining eggs, adding 25g (1 oz) of the flour mixture each time you beat one in.

7.   Fold in the remaining flour, the fruit mixture, lemon juice, treacle, and brandy.

8.   Spoon the batter into the greased tin and smooth the top with the spoon.

9.   Place the tin in the oven, and bake for 3 to 3½ hours, or until the top is pale brown. Stick a thin skewer into the centre of the cake. If no crumbs stick to it when it is removed, the cake is ready to come out of the oven.

10.   Let it cool in the tin before removing it to serve.

Makes 1 cake.

Marzipan Dates

1 egg
3 drops almond essence
110g (4 oz) ground almonds
55g (2 oz) castor sugar
55g (2 oz) icing sugar
1 box dessert dates
Additional castor sugar for coating

1. In a small bowl, beat the egg lightly and mix in the almond essence.

2. Add the almonds, castor sugar, and icing sugar, and mix until the ingredients form a smooth, firm dough.

3. Gather the dough together and place it on a clean work surface. Sprinkle it with some of the extra castor sugar, and knead it a bit to form the marzipan. Do not over mix it or it will become slippery and difficult to handle.

4. Remove the stones from the dates as carefully as possible with a small, sharp knife.

5. Break off small pieces of the marzipan and form them into little egg shapes that will fit inside the dates where the stones were. Stuff each date with one piece of marzipan.

6. Roll the dates in the remaining castor sugar and serve.

Frosted Fruits

Brightly coloured fruit, such as pears, grapes, and apples
2 egg whites (see page 99 to learn how to separate an egg)
Castor sugar

1. Wash and polish the fruit with a tea towel.

2. In a small bowl, lightly beat the egg white with a fork.

3. Cut a large square of foil and place a small pile of sugar on top.

4. Dip a small paint brush in the egg white and "paint" the fruit, making streaks of egg white over the surface. You do not have to cover the whole surface.

5. Quickly roll the fruit in the sugar, and place on a separate plate to dry. Work with 1 piece of fruit or 1 bunch of grapes at a time and allow each to dry completely before serving.

Apple Raisin Delight

1 large cooking apple
55g (2 oz) butter
25g (1 oz) cornflour
110ml (4 fl oz) water
225g (8 oz) raisins
110g (4 oz) chopped walnuts
½ tsp cinnamon
¼ tsp cloves
¼ tsp nutmeg
85g (3 oz) brown sugar
⅛ tsp salt
Double cream, whipped cream, or vanilla ice-cream
   (optional)
Walnuts or pecans (optional)

1. Wash the apple, cut it in half, and remove the core and seeds. Cut the halves into quarters, and then into bite-size pieces. Put the apple pieces aside for the moment.

2. Melt the butter in a medium-sized saucepan on the cooker, over low heat.

3. Add the chopped apple pieces, and stir them in the hot butter until they are slightly browned.

4. Add the cornflour, water, raisins, and walnuts. Stir, cooking slowly for 5 minutes over medium heat, until the mixture thickens.

5. Add the cinnamon, cloves, nutmeg, sugar, and salt. Cook until the sugar melts.

6. Let the mixture cool slightly before serving. Serve with cream, whipped cream, or vanilla ice-cream. Sprinkle with walnuts or pecans, if you wish.

Makes 2 servings.

Ginger Plum Cake

450g (1 lb) tin of plums (or peaches or apricots)
1 packet gingerbread mix
½ tsp salt
110g (4 oz) chopped walnuts or pecans
225g (8 oz) dark or golden raisins
Lemon Cream Icing (recipe follows) or whipped cream or
   vanilla ice-cream

1. Heat oven to Gas Mark 5/190°C/375°F.

2. Grease and flour a tall sided cake tin.

3. Open the tin of plums. Drain and save the plum juice or syrup, and chop up half of the plums.

4. In a large bowl, prepare the gingerbread mix according to the directions on the packet. You may wish to substitute half of the liquid (water or milk) called for with the plum juice. Do NOT pour the mix into a baking tin or bake it yet.

5. To the gingerbread mixture, add the plums you chopped, the salt, nuts, and raisins.

6. Pour mixture into baking tin. Bake for 50 to 55 minutes, or until a toothpick inserted in the centre comes out clean.

7. Let stand for 30 minutes to cool. Have an adult help you remove the cake from the tin—it's tricky.

8. Top with vanilla ice-cream, whipped cream, or Lemon Cream Icing (recipe follows).

Makes 1 cake.

Lemon Cream Icing

55g (2 oz) butter   25ml (1 fl oz) milk
110g (4 oz) sugar   25ml (1 fl oz) lemon juice
55g (2 oz) cornflour

1. Combine the butter, sugar, cornflour, and milk in a small saucepan.

2. Place the saucepan on the cooker over medium to medium-high heat, and stir the mixture constantly, until it boils. Then boil it for 1 minute.

3. Stir in the lemon juice.

4. Pour the hot icing over the ginger plum cake, and serve.

Makes enough icing for 1 cake.

Red and White Christmas Balls

10 small, round, hard, red-and-white peppermint boiled sweets
55g (2 oz) sugar
2 drops red food colouring
2 drops green food colouring
2 scoops vanilla ice-cream

1. Put the peppermint sweets in a small plastic or paper bag, and ask an adult to help you crush them with a hammer. Be careful not to pound the sweets too hard or the bag may break.

2. Put 25g (1 oz) sugar and the red food colouring in a small bowl. Stir the sugar until the food colouring is mixed in. Add more food colouring, if desired.

3. In another small bowl, place the remaining sugar and the green food colouring. Stir the sugar until the food colouring is mixed in. Add more food colouring, if desired.

4. Using an ice-cream scooper, place 1 scoop vanilla ice-cream in each of two serving bowls.

5. Decorate each ice-cream scoop with crushed peppermints and the coloured sugars.

Makes 2 servings.

Christmas Biscuits You Can Decorate

85ml (3 fl oz) honey
110g (4 oz) sugar
85g (3 oz) soft butter
1 egg
1 tsp vanilla extract
675g (1½ lbs) plain flour
1 tsp baking soda
1 tsp salt
Raisins, fruitgums, coloured sugar, or sprinkles for decoration

1. In a large bowl, thoroughly mix together the honey, sugar, butter, egg, and vanilla extract.

2. In another bowl, mix together the flour, baking soda, and salt.

3. Next, mix 110g (4 oz) of the flour mixture into the butter mixture. Use a spatula to scrape the sides of the bowl. When the flour is mixed in, add another 110g (4 oz) and mix that in.

4. Repeat step 3 until all the flour and butter are mixed together in the same bowl and well blended. The biscuit dough should be stiff.

5. Shape the dough into a ball, wrap it in a polythene bag, and chill it for 1 hour.

6. Heat the oven to Gas Mark 5/190°C/375°F.

7. Lightly grease a baking tray.

8. Divide the dough into 3 portions. Return 2 of the portions to the refrigerator.

9. Place a little extra flour on your work surface and sprinkle some on your rolling pin. Then roll out the dough until it is about ½cm (⅛ in) thick. You can use a ruler to measure it.

10. Cut the dough into different shapes with biscuit cutters.

11. Place the biscuits on the baking tray.

12. Repeat steps 9, 10, and 11 with the remaining dough.

13. Now the biscuits are ready to decorate with the raisins, fruitgums, or coloured sugar. If you want to ice your biscuits, you should do it after they are baked.

14. Bake the biscuits for 6 to 8 minutes.

15. Then remove the baking tray from the oven, and let the biscuits cool on the tray for about 2 minutes before removing them to a wire rack to cool completely.

Makes 60 biscuits.

Gingerbread Men

55g (2 oz) butter
110g (4 oz) white or firmly packed brown sugar
100ml (4 fl oz) dark molasses
55ml (2 fl oz) water
675g (1½ lbs) plain flour
½ tsp salt
½ tsp baking powder

½ tsp powdered cloves
¾ tsp powdered ginger
¼ tsp nutmeg
½ tsp cinnamon
Raisins

1. In a large bowl, blend together the butter and sugar until creamy.

2. Add the molasses and sugar and mix well.

3. In another bowl, stir together the flour, salt, baking powder, cloves, ginger, nutmeg, and cinnamon.

4. Add ⅓ of the flour mixture to the molasses mixture and mix well. Add half of the remaining flour mixture and mix well again. Then add the rest and mix well again.

5. Form the dough into a ball and wrap it in a polythene bag.

6. Chill it in the refrigerator for at least an hour.

7. Heat oven to Gas Mark 4/180°C/350°F.

8. Lightly grease a baking tray.

9. Divide dough into three portions. Put two of the portions back in the refrigerator, until you are ready to use them.

10. Roll out a portion of dough on a lightly floured board, with a lightly floured rolling pin. (If the flour does not stick to the pin, smear a few drops of vegetable oil on it first, then add the flour.) Roll the dough until it is very flat, about ½cm (⅛ in) thick. You can measure its thickness with a ruler. Biscuits that are too thick may not hold together well after baking.

11. Cut the dough with a gingerbread man biscuit cutter that has been dipped in flour.

12. Repeat steps 10 and 11 with the remaining dough.

13. With a wide spatula, place the biscuits on the prepared baking tray. Decorate the biscuits before baking with the raisins. You can make each gingerbread man look different by bending its arms or legs a little; that way, one gingerbread man can be running or waving to you, as he comes out of the oven.

14. Bake the biscuits for 8 to 10 minutes.

15. Remove from oven and allow to cool slightly. Then remove them from the baking tray and cool them on a wire rack. After the biscuits are baked, you can decorate them with icing.

Makes about 30 biscuits.

Part III

CELEBRATING CHRISTMAS:

FAVOURITE STORIES AND CAROLS

FAVOURITE CHRISTMAS STORIES

THE TAILOR OF GLOUCESTER

BY BEATRIX POTTER

(abridged)

I.

Back in the days when gentlemen wore white powdered wigs and fine coats of silk and taffeta, there lived a tailor in the city of Gloucester. In the window of a little shop on Westgate Street, he sat cross-legged on a table, from morning till dark.

All day long while the light lasted, the tailor sewed and snippeted. But although he sewed fine silk for his neighbours, he himself was very, very poor—a little old man in spectacles, with a pinched face, old crooked fingers, and a suit of threadbare clothes.

He cut his coats without wasting anything, and often remarked that the small snippets left on the table would only be good for making little vests for mice.

One bitter cold day near Christmas

© Cathy Christy O'Connor

time, the tailor began to make a coat. It was to be a special coat of cherry-coloured, corded silk, embroidered with pansies and roses, with a cream-coloured satin vest. The Mayor of Gloucester would be wearing it at his wedding on Christmas Day.

The tailor wanted this coat to be the most beautiful and perfect ever made. If the mayor were pleased with it, perhaps the tailor would be asked to make coats for other gentlemen as well.

The tailor worked and worked on the coat. He measured the silk and cut it and shaped it, and worked until the snowflakes came down against the window panes and shut out the light. By then, all the pieces of silk and satin lay cut out on the table.

There were pieces for the coat and vest, as well as for pockets, flaps, and cuffs; even the buttons were in order. The tailor would stitch the buttonholes in a cherry-coloured, twisted silk thread, called "twist." He had everything ready to sew the next morning—well, almost ready. All that was missing was a single skein of twist to stitch the last buttonhole.

That evening, the tailor came out of his shop, fastened the window, and locked the door. No one lived there at night but little brown mice. All the old houses in Gloucester had mice. There were little mouse staircases, secret trap doors, and passageways through which the mice made their way from house to house.

The tailor came out of his shop and shuffled home through the snow. He lived in only the kitchen of a small house, for that was all the tailor could afford to rent. His sole companion was his cat, Simpkin, who was very fond of catching mice.

"Meeow?" said Simpkin, as the tailor opened the door.

The tailor replied, "Simpkin, we shall make our fortune with the Mayor's coat, but right now I am worn out. Take these—my last four pennies—and go to the market. Buy a penny's worth of bread, a penny's worth of milk, and a penny's worth of sausages.

"And, oh, Simpkin," he added, "with the last penny, buy me a skein of cherry-coloured twist. I must have the twist or I cannot finish the coat!"

Simpkin went out, and the tailor, feeling chilled, sat down by the fireplace and thought of the wonderful coat.

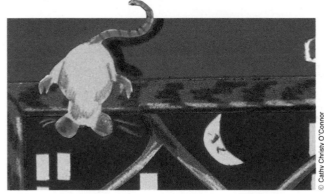

© Cathy Christy O'Connor

II.

A sound startled the tailor from his thoughts. From the dresser at the other side of the kitchen came little noises—"Tip tap, tip tap, tip tap tip!"

"Now what can that be?" asked the Tailor of Gloucester, jumping up from his chair. The dresser was covered with little china pots and bowls, willow-patterned plates, teacups, and mugs.

The tailor crossed the kitchen and stood beside the dresser, listening, and peering through his spectacles. Again, from under a teacup, came those funny little noises—"Tip tap, tip tap, tip tap tip!"

"This is very peculiar," said the Tailor of Gloucester, and he lifted up the teacup, which was upside down.

Out stepped a little lady mouse, and she made a curtsy to the tailor! Then she hopped down off the dresser and slipped beneath the panelling near the floor.

The tailor was on his way back to his chair by the fire, when there came other little noises from the dresser. He went back and turned over another teacup, which was upside down. Out stepped a little gentleman mouse, who bowed to the tailor!

Then, from all over the dresser, came a chorus of little tappings—"Tip, tap, tip tap, tip tap tip!" And out from under teacups, bowls, and basins stepped more little mice, who hopped off the dresser and slipped under the panelling near the floor.

But the tailor was thinking too hard about the coat for the Mayor of Gloucester to pay much attention to the mice. "Twenty-one buttonholes of cherry-coloured silk!" he exclaimed. "To be finished in four days' time."

Then the tailor had another thought: "Was I wise to entrust my last bit of money to Simpkin? Suppose he forgets the twist!" Then the tailor wondered if he should have let the mice loose—Simpkin had no doubt caught them himself to enjoy later.

But the tailor's thoughts soon turned back to his coat, and he began speaking of it out loud to himself. The little mice came out and listened as he spoke, taking note of the pattern planned for the wonderful coat. Then all at once they ran away, scurrying together through the passages beneath the floor. They squeaked and called to one another, as they ran from house to house. Not one mouse was left in the tailor's kitchen, when Simpkin came back from his errands.

Simpkin was in a bad mood, for he did not like the snow, and there was snow in his ears. Sniffing the kitchen for his supper, he immediately noticed there were no mice left on the dresser. "Hmmph!" he thought. He put down the bread, sausages, and milk—but he hid the other little parcel in a teapot on the dresser.

"Simpkin," said the tailor, "where is my twist?"

If Simpkin had been able to talk, he would have asked: "Where are my MICE?"

The tailor went sadly off to bed, while Simpkin spent the night searching through the kitchen for his mice.

All the next day the tailor was ill, and the next day, and the next. In his feverish dreams, he cried out, "No more twist!"

III.

On Christmas Eve, and very late at night, the moon rose over the roofs and chimneys of Gloucester. There were no lights on in any windows, and no sounds from any homes. The city was fast asleep under the snow.

And still Simpkin wanted his mice.

Now, it is said that in the hours between Christmas Eve and dawn on Christmas morning all beasts and animals can talk. That night, when the Cathedral clock struck twelve, Simpkin wandered out of the tailor's door and into the snowy street.

The sound of merry roosters singing Christmas rhymes was ringing through the air. Cats were dancing and singing in attics across the way. The sparrows sang of Christmas pies, and even the robins awoke from their sleep and began to sing.

All this merriment only annoyed Simpkin, who was hungry and looking for food. He wandered over to the tailor's shop, where light was glowing from the window. Creeping up, he saw that the

© Cathy Christy O'Connor

shop was lit with many tiny candles. There was a snippeting of scissors, and snappeting of thread, and little mouse voices were singing gaily as they went about their work.

"Mew! Mew!" interrupted Simpkin, and he scratched at the door. But the key was under the tailor's pillow, so he could not get in. The little mice only laughed and tried another tune—

"Three little mice sat down to spin;
Kitty passed by and she peeped in.
'What are you at, my fine little men?'
'Making coats for gentlemen.'
'Shall I come in and cut off your threads?'
'Oh, no, Miss Kitty, you'd bite off our
   heads!' "

"Mew! scratch! scratch!" scuffled Simpkin on the window sill. Inside, the little mice sprang up and barred the window shutters and shut out Simpkin. But through the nicks in the shutters Simpkin could hear the click of thimbles. At one point he heard them shout in little twittering voices, "No more twist! No more twist!"

Simpkin turned away and went home, thinking about the mice and how they were helping the poor tailor. When he got home, Simpkin found the tailor without fever, sleeping peacefully.

Then Simpkin went on tip-toe and took a little parcel of silk out of the teapot. He felt quite ashamed of his badness, compared with those good little mice!

When the tailor awoke in the morning, the first thing he saw was a skein of cherry-coloured twisted silk on his patchwork blanket, and beside his bed stood the repentant Simpkin!

The sun was shining on the snow as the tailor got up and dressed. He went out into the street, with Simpkin running before him. The starlings whistled on the chimney stacks, but they sang their own little noises, not the words they had sung in the night.

"Alas," said the tailor, "I have my twist but no more time. This is Christmas Day and the Mayor will be married at noon! He'll wonder why his cherry-coloured coat is not finished."

He unlocked the door of the little shop on Westgate Street, and Simpkin ran in, as if expecting something. But there was no one there! Not even one little brown mouse!

The boards were swept clean; the little ends of thread and the little silk snippets were all tidied away.

But on the table—oh joy! The tailor gave a shout, for there—where he had left plain cuttings of silk—lay the most beautiful coat and embroidered satin vest that would ever be worn by a Mayor of Gloucester.

There were roses and pansies on the coat facings, and the vest was trimmed with poppies and cornflowers. Everything was finished, except for one single buttonhole; and on that buttonhole was pinned a scrap of paper with these words—in teeny weeny writing—"No More Twist."

There began the luck of the Tailor of Gloucester. He grew quite stout and quite rich. He made the most wonderful coats and vests for all the wealthy merchants of Gloucester, and for all the fine gentlemen living in the countryside nearby.

No one had ever seen such ruffles, or such embroidered cuffs and folds! But his buttonholes were the greatest triumph.

The stitches of those buttonholes were so neat—*so* neat—it was a wonder they could be stitched by an old man in spectacles, with crooked old fingers and a tailor's thimble. The stitches were so very small, in fact, they looked as if they had been made by little mice!

IS THERE A FATHER CHRISTMAS?

(Edited and abridged)

It sometimes happens that people begin to wonder if the things they believe in are really true. One of these things is Father Christmas. Have you ever wondered if there really is a Father Christmas?

In 1908, a little girl in New York City was so curious about whether or not there was a Father Christmas, she wrote a letter to the local newspaper, the New York *Sun*. The girl, Virginia O'Hanlon, hoped that the people in charge of the newspaper might be able to answer her question. She wrote:

Dear Editor:

I am eight years old.

Some of my friends say there is no Father Christmas.

Papa says, "If you see it in the *Sun*, it's so."

Please tell me the truth, is there a Father Christmas?

Virginia O'Hanlon
115 West 95th Street

One of the New York *Sun's* editors, a man named Francis P. Church, wrote Virginia:

Virginia, your little friends are wrong. Unfortunately, we live in an age when people only believe in what they can see and understand.

Yes, Virginia, there is a Father Christ-mas. He exists as certainly as love and generosity and devotion exist. Alas! How dreary the world would be if there were no Father Christmas! It would be as dreary as if there were no Virginias.

Not believe in Father Christmas! You might as well not believe in fairies! You might get your papa to hire men to watch in all the chimneys on Christmas Eve to catch Father Christmas, but even if they did not see Father Christmas coming down, what would that prove? Nobody sees Father Christmas, but that is no sign there is no Father Christmas.

The most real things in the world are those that neither children nor men can see. Did you ever see fairies dancing on the lawn? Of course not, but that's no proof that they are not there. Nobody can conceive or imagine all the wonders there are in the world that we have never seen or never can see.

Only faith, imagination, poetry, love, and romance can help us see and appreciate the world's heavenly beauty and mystery. Is it all real? Ah, Virginia, in all this world there is nothing else real and eternal.

No Father Christmas! Thank God he lives, and he lives forever. A thousand years from now, Virginia, nay, ten times ten thousand years from now, he will continue to make glad the heart of childhood.

THE LEGEND OF BEFANA

Many, many years ago a woman named Befana lived by herself on a small country road. The woman led a simple life and never wondered what the next day might bring.

One evening, as Befana was sweeping her cottage, she suddenly stopped and listened. Outside, in the distance, she thought she heard a trumpet. She went over to the window and looked out.

Riding up the road were three magnificent men in flowing robes and turbans. They were preceded by a young page, who was blowing his trumpet to announce their way.

Befana could hardly believe her eyes.

Imagine such splendid, royal men riding up her little road! Their horses were as tall and proud as any horses could be; and by the bright-coloured silks that made up the kings' robes, Befana guessed they came from the Orient, where she had heard such riches existed.

To her surprise, the kings rode right up to her house and stopped outside her door. Their golden gowns shimmered in the evening light, and the jewels on their crowns shone like stars.

"Come in, Your Highnesses," said Befana, curtsying.

"No thank you, good woman," said the first king. "We've been following a bright star that is leading us to a newborn King, who will be the Saviour of all the people."

"But we seem to have lost our way," added the second king.

Befana looked puzzled. "I'm sorry, but I don't know how to help you," she said.

"Join us in our search," said the third king. "Come help us find Him. When we do, we will offer the Child gifts and rejoice in His birth."

Befana looked up the road, where the kings and page were headed. It was dark outside. She was tired and it was suppertime.

"Couldn't we go tomorrow?" she asked.

"No," said the kings. "We must not linger."

All Befana had to ride on was an old brown donkey, and he needed a good night's rest. Besides, she just was not ready to leave her cottage while it was in such disorder.

"Tomorrow," said Befana. "I promise I'll join you then. Tonight, I'd like to finish my sweeping."

The three kings said, "Very well, then. If you cannot come now, we must be on our way." With that, they got back on their horses and disappeared up the road and into the night.

Befana returned to her sweeping, and when she had finished, she sat down to a quiet dinner of grapes and barley cakes. She thought again of the three kings and of the Child they were seeking.

"It must be no ordinary Babe, if such important men are looking for him," she said to herself.

Befana did not sleep well that night. At the first light of dawn, she left her spotless cottage and headed up the road on her donkey, determined to find the three kings.

Befana rode and rode and asked everyone along the way if they had seen the three kings, or heard of the whereabouts of the newborn King. But everyone she asked just shook their heads, and Befana rode onward. She never returned to her cottage.

Years passed and Befana grew old. She realized that she might never find the Child and felt sorry that she had never seen Him or given Him any presents. To make up for that, she gathered little sweets and trinkets whenever she could and put them in a large bag. Befana wanted to give these treats secretly to every child in the land.

On the next anniversary of the three kings' visit to her cottage, Befana carried out her plan. On that twelfth night after Christmas, every door in every village miraculously stood open. No one awoke as Befana left her presents at each house. Befana went everywhere—up and down main roads and forgotten streets. She went quickly and quietly, until her work was done. As the sun crept up over the horizon, Befana felt sleepy, warm, and happier than ever before.

Hundreds of years have passed since then, but many children in Italy and Russia still await her visit. In that time, Befana has got to know many, many children. For the naughty ones, she leaves behind coal and stones, and hopes they will be better next year. But for all good children, Befana brings a special gift.

What Befana receives in return is the joy and love of giving, year after year.

Illustration by Thomas Nast

A VISIT
FROM ST. NICHOLAS
(The Night Before Christmas)

BY CLEMENT CLARKE MOORE

T was the night before Christmas, when all through the house
Not a creature was stirring, not even a mouse.
The stockings were hung by the chimney with care,
In hopes that St. Nicholas soon would be there.

The children were nestled all snug in their beds,
While visions of sugar plums danced in their heads;
And mamma in her kerchief, and I in my cap,
Had just settled our brains for a long winter's nap—
When out on the lawn there arose such a clatter,
I sprang from my bed to see what was the matter.
Away to the window I flew like a flash,
Tore open the shutters and threw up the sash.

The moon, on the breast of the new-fallen snow,
Gave a lustre of midday to objects below;
When what to my wondering eyes should appear,
But a miniature sleigh and eight tiny reindeer,
With a little old driver, so lively and quick
I knew in a moment it must be St. Nick.
More rapid than eagles his coursers they came,
And he whistled and shouted and called them by name:
"Now, Dasher! now, Dancer! now, Prancer and Vixen!
On, Comet! on, Cupid! on, Donder and Blitzen!
To the top of the porch, to the top of the wall!
Now dash away, dash away, dash away all!"
As dry leaves that before the wild hurricane fly,
When they meet with an obstacle, mount to the sky,
So, up to the house-top the courses they flew,
With a sleigh full of toys—and St. Nicholas too.

And then in a twinkling I heard on the roof
The prancing and pawing of each little hoof.
As I drew in my head and was turning around,
Down the chimney St. Nicholas came with a bound.
He was dressed all in fur from his head to his foot,
And his clothes were all tarnished with ashes and soot;
A bundle of toys he had flung on his back,
And he looked like a peddler just opening his pack.

Illustration by Thomas Nast

His eyes, how they twinkled! his dimples, how merry!
His cheeks were like roses, his nose like a cherry;
His droll little mouth was drawn up like a bow,
And the beard on his chin was as white as the snow.
The stump of a pipe he held tight in his teeth,
And the smoke, it encircled his head like a wreath.
He had a broad face, and a little round belly
That shook, when he laughed, like a bowl full of jelly.

He was chubby and plump—a right jolly old elf—
And I laughed when I saw him, in spite of myself.
A wink of his eye and a twist of his head
Soon gave me to know I had nothing to dread.
He spoke not a word, but went straight to his work,
And filled all the stockings; then turned with a jerk,
And laying his finger aside of his nose,
And giving a nod, up the chimney he rose.

He sprang to his sleigh, to his team gave a whistle,
And away they all flew like the down of a thistle;
But I heard him exclaim, ere he drove out of sight:
"Happy Christmas to all, and to all a good night!"

Illustration by Thomas Nast

A CHRISTMAS CAROL

BY CHARLES DICKENS

(abridged)

Photographs from "A Christmas Carol": Courtesy Entertainment Partners/IBM/George C. Scott; Photography by David James.

Part One:

Ebenezer Scrooge

Ebenezer Scrooge was a squeezing, wrenching, grasping, scraping, clutching, miserable old sinner! No heat could warm him, no cold could chill him, and no wind that blew was more bitter than he.

Scrooge's only friend had been an old, crabby man just like him. That man was his partner, Jacob Marley, but Marley had been as dead as a doornail for seven years. Scrooge was all alone, but he liked it that way.

One cold, bleak Christmas Eve afternoon, Scrooge sat in his office counting his money. In a dismal little room behind him, a poor clerk named Bob Cratchit was trying to warm his hands over the single candle that lit his desk. Suddenly, Scrooge's nephew, Fred, burst cheerily through the front door.

"A Merry Christmas, uncle!" Fred said.

"Bah!" said Scrooge. "Humbug!"

" 'Humbug?' Uncle, you don't mean that!"

"Yes, I do," said Scrooge—and he did. To him, every day was meant for making money. Christmas time, the season for spending money and extending human kindness, was sheer nonsense to Scrooge.

Still, Fred was not discouraged, and he invited his uncle to a Christmas party the following afternoon. That only angered Scrooge.

"Good afternoon!" he snapped, shooing Fred away.

"Merry Christmas, uncle!" Fred called brightly as he left, but Scrooge just slammed the door.

At closing time, Scrooge glanced up at his clerk, Bob Cratchit, who was tugging a thin, white shawl around his shoulders. Cratchit was too poor to buy himself a real coat.

"I suppose you want tomorrow off," said Scrooge with a scowl.

"Yes. Please, sir," said Cratchit. "It's only once a year, sir."

"All right," grumbled Scrooge, "but be here all the earlier the *next* morning."

The clerk promised he would and closed the door behind him.

That evening, as Scrooge was unlocking the door to his gloomy house, he noticed something strange about the knocker on the door. There, on the very same plain knocker that Scrooge had seen every day of his life was old Jacob Marley's face!

The face was not angry or ferocious. It just stared at Scrooge through its ghostly spectacles. Scrooge stared back, and the face disappeared.

"Bah! Humbug!" said Scrooge, and closed the door with a bang.

Part Two: *Marley's Ghost*

Scrooge went upstairs. The house was dark, but he did not mind, because keeping it dark was cheaper than lighting candles. Still, Scrooge was bothered by the memory of Marley's face upon the knocker. He closed his bedroom door and double-locked himself in, just to be safe. After putting on his night clothes, he settled into a chair near the fire to take his nightly bowl of gruel.

Suddenly, an old bell that hung in the room began to swing. Soon, it rang out loudly, as did every bell in the house. Then, to Scrooge's astonishment and dread, a clanking noise began, as if someone were dragging a heavy chain.

Scrooge trembled in his chair, as the clanking came up the stairs, straight towards his door, and then straight *through* the door! And a spectre passed into the room before his eyes. As it did, the flame in the fireplace shot up, as if crying out, "I know him—it's Marley's ghost!"

It was Marley's face, all right. The same pigtail, waistcoat, and boots—yet his body was transparent and chains hung round about him.

"Hmmph!" said Scrooge, as bitter and cold as ever. "What do you want with me?"

"Much!" said the spirit. It was Marley's voice, no doubt about it.

"Who are you?" demanded Scrooge.

"In life, I was your partner, Jacob Marley," said the ghost, sitting down in a chair across from Scrooge. "But you don't believe in me, do you?"

"No, I don't," said Scrooge.

With that, Marley moaned loudly and rattled his chains.

Scrooge was horrified. "Mercy! Dreadful apparition, why do you trouble me?" he cried.

Marley spoke solemnly. "It is required of every living person to walk among friends and strangers, to be generous and kind," the ghost said. "Because I did not do this in life, I am condemned to do so in death. I can never stop and never rest. Many weary journeys lie before me."

"But why do you come to me?" asked Scrooge.

"Oh, blind man!" shouted Marley. "You, who have shunned as many of life's opportunities as I did! The same terrible fate awaits you, too. But I come here tonight to warn you that you have a chance of escaping this."

In his strange and shadowy voice, Marley told Scrooge that he would be haunted by Three Spirits. The first would come when the church bell tolled one o'clock. The second would come the next night at the same hour; and the third, at the last stroke of midnight on the next night.

"Look to see me no more!" said Marley. "And remember what has passed between us." With that, he disappeared.

Scrooge tried to say, "Humbug!", but stopped at the first syllable, suddenly exhausted. He fell into bed and was instantly fast asleep.

Part Three: *The First of the Three Spirits*

The room was pitch black when Scrooge awoke. Outside, the church bell tolled a deep, dull, melancholy one o'clock.

Instantly, light flashed into the room and a strange figure appeared at Scrooge's bedside. He was small and looked like a child—almost. His hair was white, as if with age, yet his skin was smooth as a flower petal. He held a branch of fresh, green holly in his hand, and on his head he wore a crown that gave off a bright, clear light. Scrooge cleared his throat.

"Are you the Spirit, sir, that I was told to expect?"

"I am! I am the Ghost of Christmas Past," said the figure.

"Long Past?" asked Scrooge.

"No. Your past. The things you will see with me are shadows of things that have

Photographs from "A Christmas Carol": Courtesy Entertainment Partners/IBM/George C. Scott; Photography by David James

been. Come! Rise and walk with me!"

The Spirit walked onto the window ledge and held out his hand for Scrooge to follow.

"But I am a mortal, and liable to fall!" cried Scrooge.

"Touch my hand," said the Spirit.

Scrooge did so and suddenly the two stood in the middle of a city. By the looks of the shop windows, it was clearly Christmas time here, too. The Ghost stopped at a certain warehouse door and asked Scrooge if he knew where they were.

"Of course! I learned my trade here!" Scrooge exclaimed. As they went inside, Scrooge was amazed to see an old gentleman in a Welsh wig, who was sitting behind a desk so high, his head nearly touched the ceiling. "Why, it's old Fezziwig! Bless his heart, he's alive again!" cried Scrooge. He called to the man, but the Spirit shook his head.

"No one can see us," said the Ghost.

Old Fezziwig laid down his pen and looked up at the clock, as it chimed seven times. He rubbed his hands, adjusted his large waistcoat, laughed heartily, and called out in a rich, fat, jolly voice, "Yo ho, there! Ebenezer! Dick!"

A young Ebenezer Scrooge came briskly in, accompanied by his fellow apprentice.

"There's Dick Wilkins!" said Scrooge to the Ghost. "He was very much attached to me. Poor Dick! Dear, dear!"

"Yo ho! No more work tonight," said Fezziwig. "It's Christmas Eve, my boys! Let's clear away and make lots of room."

In a minute, the furniture was cleared away, the floor was swept and watered, the lamps were trimmed, fuel was heaped upon the fire; and the warehouse was as snug and warm and bright a ballroom as you would ever want to see on a winter's night.

The fiddler came and went up to the lofty desk, which he quickly made into a lively, musical balcony. The guests arrived: the jolly Mrs. Fezziwig and her three lovable daughters; six young gentlemen; the housemaid and her cousin, the baker; the cook and her friend, and the milkman. Some were shy, some were bold, but as the music started up, away they all went! Twenty couples dancing at

once, never minding a wrong step here and a clumsy twirl there.

There were dances and more dances. There was cake, too, and a huge roast beef. There were mince pies and plenty of beer. But the high point of the evening came when Fezziwig and Mrs. Fezziwig stood up to dance. They were a first-rate couple, spinning 'round and 'round. Everyone cheered, and then joined in the dancing themselves.

The lovely, little ball broke up at eleven o'clock, with Fezziwig and his wife exchanging heartfelt Christmas wishes with their guests as they left.

"Imagine!" said the Ghost. "Such a small thing could make those silly folks so happy. Why, the old man spent but a few pounds on his party—does he deserve so much praise?"

"It isn't that," said Scrooge, as heated by the remark as young Ebenezer himself would have been. "The happiness old Fezziwig gave is as great as if it cost a fortune. I wish..."

"What?" asked the Spirit.

"It's nothing. I'd just like to say a word or two to my clerk right now. That's all," said Scrooge.

In a flash, the Spirit whisked the two of them off to a different scene. There was Ebenezer, older now, in the prime of his life. He sat beside a fair young girl, who was crying.

"You've changed," the girl was saying. "You fear the world too much, and all you want is money and gain. You could never love a poor girl like me. I only hope your money can comfort you in hard times, the way I would have."

Ebenezer started to protest, but the girl stopped him. "Goodbye, Ebenezer!" she said. "I'll always love the man you once were."

"Spirit! Remove me from this place!"

cried Scrooge. And suddenly Scrooge was in bed, in a deep, heavy sleep.

Part Four: *The Second of the Three Spirits*

When Scrooge awoke, his bedroom and the adjoining sitting room had undergone a surprising transformation. The walls were thick with holly, mistletoe, and ivy. A mighty blaze was roaring in the fireplace, and heaped upon the floor was an enormous feast. There were turkeys, geese, sausages, plum puddings, barrels of oysters, cherry-cheeked apples and luscious pears, cakes, and great bowls of punch.

On Scrooge's couch sat a Giant, glorious to see. He raised a glowing torch in his hand to shed its light on Scrooge, who peeked out from his bedroom door.

"Come in, come in!" urged the Giant. "I am the Ghost of Christmas Present."

Scrooge shuffled in, wearing slippers. "Lead me where you will, Spirit," he said. "Last night I learned a lesson that is working now. I am ready to learn from what you have to show me."

"Touch my robe!" said the Spirit.

Scrooge did as he was told, and the room and all its contents vanished. They stood in the city streets on a snowy Christmas morning. Invisible, the two went directly to Bob Cratchit's humble home.

In the kitchen, Mrs. Cratchit and young Belinda, Martha, and Peter Cratchit stood boiling, mashing, sweetening, and stirring the various dishes for the Christmas meal. Meanwhile, Bob Cratchit was seating one son, Tiny Tim, beside him at the corner of the table.

Poor Tiny Tim was crippled, and bore a little crutch. It was easy to see that Bob adored this son and had faith that he would grow to be strong and healthy.

When everything was hissing hot and ready to be served, the family gathered around the dining table. The Cratchits were not a handsome family; they were not well dressed; and they were poor. But none of that dimmed the excitement of sitting down with one another at Christmas dinner.

There was a breathless pause around the table, as Mrs. Cratchit raised the carving knife to cut the goose. When she did, and the gush of stuffing issued forth, a murmur of delight arose among all the Cratchits; even Tiny Tim feebly cried, "Hurrah!"

The goose was not large, but to the Cratchits, it was fit for a king; along with mashed potatoes and applesauce, it was enough dinner for the whole family.

The meal's grand finale, of course, was the plum pudding, a dessert of utmost importance to any Christmas dinner. To the Cratchits, the thought each year that the pudding would be less than perfect was enough to set each family member on the edge of his seat. But they should not have worried.

It was a wonderful pudding! It was round, like a speckled cannon ball, so hard and firm; it blazed in an eighth of an inch of brandy, with a sprig of Christmas holly stuck in the top. Everybody had something to say about the pudding, but nobody said or thought that it was a small pudding for a large family. Any Cratchit would have blushed to hint at such a thing.

After dinner, Bob Cratchit drew his family around the fireplace, a small glass of punch in his hand. He held the glass high and said, "A Merry Christmas to us all, my dears. God bless us!" And all the family echoed this sentiment.

"God bless us every one!" said Tiny Tim. He sat close to his father, upon his little stool. Bob took Tim's withered little hand in his, and held it as if he feared that the child would be taken from him.

"Another toast," said Bob, "to Mr. Scrooge, the Founder of the Feast!"

"The Founder of the Feast indeed!" cried Mrs. Cratchit, reddening. "If he were here, I'd give him a piece of my mind to feast upon!"

"My dear," said Bob, "the children! Christmas day."

Scrooge looked startled at hearing himself talked about that way. It disturbed him that his very name seemed to have cast a heavy shadow over the Cratchit family's merry afternoon. But when the gloom passed away, the family seemed ten times merrier than they had before.

The Cratchits were happy, grateful, and pleased with one another. They looked even happier in the bright sprinkling of the Spirit's torch at parting. Scrooge looked at all of them, especially Tiny Tim, until the happy scene faded from his sight.

In the distance, the church clock struck twelve. Scrooge looked about him and saw that the Ghost had disappeared. But lifting up his eyes, Scrooge saw a solemn Phantom, draped and hooded, coming toward him like a mist along the ground.

Part Five: *The Last of the Spirits*

The Phantom approached slowly, gravely, and silently. It was shrouded in a deep, black garment that concealed its head, face, and form. It left nothing visible save one outstretched hand. Scrooge knew nothing more of this gloomy, mysterious spirit, for it neither spoke nor moved.

"Am I in the presence of the Ghost of Christmas Yet to Come?" asked Scrooge, falling to his knees. "I fear you more than any spectre I have seen so far. But I know your purpose is to do me good; since I hope to live a new life after this, I am prepared to join you now. And I do it with a thankful heart."

The Spirit gave no reply. The hand was pointed straight before them.

"Lead on, Spirit!" said Scrooge.

Quickly, they were in the heart of the city. The Spirit stopped beside a knot of businessmen and pointed to them. Scrooge went toward them to listen to their talk.

"When did he die?" asked one man.

"Last night, I believe," said another.

"Why, what was the matter with him?" asked a third.

Photographs from "A Christmas Carol"; Courtesy Entertainment Partners/IBM/George C. Scott; Photography by David James.

"Who knows?" said the second man, with a yawn. "I thought he'd never die."

"And what did he do with his money?" asked the first.

The second man replied with a laugh, "All I know is—he didn't leave it to me!"

The men parted, chuckling among themselves.

Scrooge did not know what to think of the conversation. He was not quite sure who had died, and why the Spirit had wanted him to listen. But when the Spirit led him to his office and Scrooge did not see himself there, he began to understand.

When the Spirit took Scrooge past his house, Scrooge saw a cleaning woman and a laundress walking out with huge bundles over their backs. From their conversation, Scrooge realized that they had taken away his curtains, blankets, and best clothes in order to sell them.

"If he'd wanted to keep them after he was dead," said the cleaning woman, "why, he'd have had somebody to look after them, instead of dying sick and alone by himself."

"It's absolutely true," said the laundress. "He deserved what he got!"

Scrooge listened to this in horror. "Spirit," he cried, "please, let me see some tenderness connected with this death!"

The Ghost conducted him to poor Bob Cratchit's house, but the scene this time was very different from the merry one he had visited earlier. Bob, Mrs. Cratchit, Peter, Belinda, and Martha were seated around the fire. They were all quiet, very quiet.

Bob was reading aloud to them, trying to be pleasant and cheerful, but not succeeding at all. His eyes were brimming with tears, which he would dash away with the back of his hand.

Scrooge saw that the little stool next to

Bob was empty. On it lay a tiny crutch. "Tiny Tim!" Scrooge exclaimed. "Oh, no, not Tiny Tim!"

The Cratchit house suddenly faded and the air grew dark and still. The Ghost of Christmas Yet to Come led Scrooge to a dismal churchyard. The Spirit stood among the graves and pointed down to one.

"Oh, Spirit, before I look upon that stone, tell me that these are only shadows of things that Might be, not of things that Will be!"

The Ghost continued to point at the grave.

"Please, Spirit, tell me that if I change my life, its end will also change. Tell me that is why you have shown me these terrible things!"

Still, the Ghost would not answer, and Scrooge crept toward the grave. The stone was marked, "Ebenezer Scrooge."

"Tell me it's not so, Spirit!" cried Scrooge. "I am not the man I was. I will honour Christmas in my heart and try to keep it all year through. I will live in the

Past, the Present, and the Future. I will not shut out the lessons the Spirits have taught me. Oh, tell me I may erase the writing on this stone!"

Scrooge held up his hands in one last prayer. As he did, the Phantom's hood and dress shrank, collapsed, and dwindled down into a bedpost.

And the bedpost was his own. The bed was his own, the room was his own. Best and happiest of all, the Time before him was his own. Scrooge was free to change his life and make it better.

Part Six: Scrooge's Christmas

Scrooge ran to the window and opened it. Outside was a bright, stirring, golden day. The church bells were ringing out the lustiest peals he had ever heard.

"What's today?" cried Scrooge, calling down to a boy in Sunday clothes.

"Today? Why, *Christmas day!*" replied the boy.

"Hurray! I haven't missed it!" exclaimed Scrooge. With that, he offered the boy a crown if he'd go down to the poultry store and buy the big prize turkey hanging in the window.

"Tell them to bring it here, so I can tell them where to take it," said Scrooge. The boy was off like a shot.

"I'll send it to Bob Cratchit's!" said Scrooge, tickled with pleasure, "and he'll never guess who sent it!"

Later that morning, Scrooge put on his best clothes and went out into the streets. People were everywhere, and Scrooge looked at everyone with a delightful smile. He looked so irresistibly pleasant that three or four good-natured fellows said, "Good morning, sir! A merry Christ-

mas to you!" And Scrooge said often afterwards, that of all the beautiful sounds he had ever heard, those words were the most beautiful in his ears.

That afternoon, Scrooge surprised his nephew, Fred, by showing up at his house for dinner.

"Why bless my soul!" cried Fred, upon seeing his uncle—and it's a wonder Fred did not shake Scrooge's arm off. It was a wonderful party of close friends. They played games and sang happily all afternoon.

The next morning Scrooge could hardly conceal his new happiness. But he greeted Bob Cratchit in his usual severe manner.

"You're late, Cratchit!" he barked.

"I'm very sorry, sir. It won't happen again, sir," said Bob.

"Now, I won't stand for this any longer! And therefore," said Scrooge, laying a hand on Bob's shoulder—and "therefore, I am about to raise your salary!"

Bob trembled and looked up.

"A merry Christmas, Bob!" laughed Scrooge. "Yes, my friend, I'll raise your salary and try to help your struggling family. We'll discuss your affairs this very afternoon. So make up the fires, Bob, and buy a second bag of coal before you do another thing!"

Scrooge was better than his word. He did it all and much, much more. And to Tiny Tim, who did NOT die, he became a second father. Some people laughed to see the change in Scrooge, but his own heart laughed, and that was quite enough for him.

It was always said that if any man knew how to keep the Christmas spirit, Ebenezer Scrooge knew how. May that truly be said of all of us! And so, as Tiny Tim was fond of saying, "God Bless Us Every One!"

© Bob Kosturko 1988

THE LEGEND OF
THE CAT

On the night of the First Christmas, the beasts and birds quickly flocked to Bethlehem to honour the Baby Jesus. Among those visitors was the Cat. Unlike most of the animals, who were somewhat noisy in their eagerness to see the Child, the Cat came quietly, on her padded paws.

While the other animals pushed forward to look in the manger, the Cat stood back shyly. Nor could she kneel in praise, as the others did, for she was too awed by the sight to move at all. When the deer, lion, pheasant, rabbit, and fox burst into a hymn to Jesus, the Cat could only make a low, nervous tremble that caught in her throat.

As the sun rose in the morning, the animals returned home to the wild, one by one. Only the Cat remained in the stable. She continued to gaze upon the beautiful Nativity scene, unwilling to go back to her home in the forest.

Mary noticed how the Cat had stayed. She looked upon the animal's proud, serious face and smiled. "I bless you, Cat," she said. "From now on, you will never have to go back to the wilderness. Instead, wherever there are warm homes and caring people, you shall be there too."

Today, the gleam in a cat's eyes still speaks of her first life in the wild; her sharp claws and wild, lonely cry at night are other reminders of that time. But just feel a cat purr sweetly in your arms, or cuddle up against your leg—and you will think of Mary's blessing of the Cat on that very First Christmas.

THE LEGEND OF ROBIN RED-BREAST

© Cathy Christy O'Connor

O n that First Christmas, it is said, the night was wrapped in a bitter chill. The small fire in the stable was nearly out, and the Mother Mary worried that her Baby would be cold. She turned to the animals about her and asked them for help.

"Could you blow on the embers," she asked the ox, "so the fire might continue to keep my Son warm?"

But the ox lay sound asleep on the stable floor and did not hear her.

Next, Mary asked the donkey to breathe life back into the fire, but the sleeping donkey did not hear Mary either. Nor did the horse or sheep. She wondered what to do.

Suddenly, Mary heard a fluttering of little wings. Looking up, she saw a plain, brown-coloured robin fly into the stall. This robin had heard Mary calling to the animals and had come to help her himself. He went over to the dying fire and flapped his wings hard.

His wings were like little bellows, huffing and puffing air onto the embers, until they glowed bright red again. He continued to fan the fire, singing all the while, until the ashes began to kindle.

With his beak, the robin picked up some fresh, dry sticks and tossed them into the fire. As he did, a flame suddenly burst forth and burned the little bird's breast a bright red. But the robin simply continued to fan the fire until it crackled brightly and warmed the entire stable. The Baby Jesus slept happily.

Mary thanked and praised the robin for all he had done. She looked tenderly at his red breast, burned by the flame, and said, "From now on, let your red breast be a blessed reminder of your noble deed."

And to this day, the robin's red breast covers his humble heart.

THE NUTCRACKER

Adapted from "The Nutcracker and the King of the Mice"

BY E.T.A. HOFFMAN

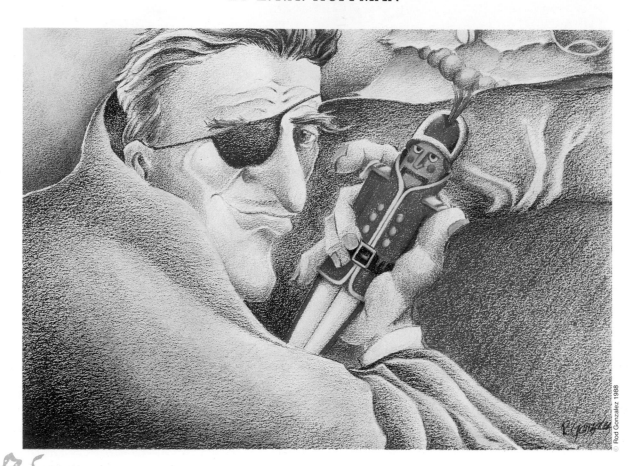

This story is the basis of a famous ballet set to the music of Peter Tchaikovsky. You may have seen this ballet around Christmas time, either on television or in a theatre. *The Nutcracker* is one of the world's most popular ballets.

I. Dr. Drosselmeyer's Surprise

It was Christmas Eve in a small, snow-covered town in Germany, many years ago. At the von Stahlbaums' home a party was in progress, and the air fairly crackled with the joy of friends and relatives gathered together. A fire blazed in the hearth; the banquet table was laden with delicious foods; and round about the Christmas tree, the children were eagerly unwrapping their gifts.

"Look—toy soliders!" cried Fritz von Stahlbaum, and he held up a blue-jacketed soldier for all to admire.

Fritz's sister, Clara, opened her present next. "Ballet shoes!" she exclaimed. "These are just what I wanted!"

The other children were equally content with their presents, and the grown-ups stood by watching, pleased and amused.

Suddenly, a strong, cold burst of wind whipped down the front hall and into the parlour where everyone was gathered. Through the door came a mysterious-looking man in a powdered wig and a thick, black cloak. The room fell silent for a moment, and the children scurried to the protection of their parents.

But Mr. and Mrs. von Stahlbaum greeted their guest heartily. "Merry Christmas, Dr. Drosselmeyer! Come in!" they said, welcoming their friend and Clara's godfather.

Everyone knew that Dr. Drosselmeyer was no ordinary doctor. He wore a patch over one eye, like a pirate, and he moved his hands swiftly—like a magician.

Dr. Drosselmeyer smiled and bowed to his hosts; he then waved to two footmen, who brought in a pair of dolls—a boy and a girl, dressed as clowns. He wound the dolls up and they sprang into a dance so lively, they seemed almost real.

"More! More!" cried the children, forgetting their fear of the doctor.

Dr. Drosselmeyer drew the children into a circle around him. From the depths of his thick, black cape he pulled out a large, wooden Nutcracker, carved and brightly painted to resemble a soldier. His jacket was scarlet, like the jaunty feather in his helmet, and he had a stiff smile on his face.

A dozen eager hands shot up at once, each child hoping to receive this beautiful toy. Dr. Drosselmeyer reached over their heads and handed the Nutcracker to Clara.

"For me?" she exclaimed, astonished to receive a second wonderful gift. She cradled the Nutcracker in her arms.

Fritz eyed his sister enviously. "Let *me* see it," he said, grabbing it out of her hands. Fritz turned and ran with it, when suddenly he tripped and fell, smacking the Nutcracker against the floor. The lovely toy lay broken and Clara burst into tears.

The evening ended shortly afterward, as tears were dried and apologies given. Before he left, Dr. Drosselmeyer picked the Nutcracker up and placed it gently under the tree. The last remaining guest went home, yawning happily, and the lights were put out one by one. Fritz and Clara were tucked into bed, and soon the whole house was fast asleep.

II. The Nutcracker and The Seven-Headed Mouse

Clara awoke in the middle of the night. She wondered where her Nutcracker was and crept out of bed to find it. The house was dark and full of shadows, as Clara stole silently downstairs to the parlour door. Peeking in, she was relieved to see the Nutcracker lying safely under the tree.

Clara wanted to take the Nutcracker upstairs with her, but the parlour felt spooky in the night; the curtains fluttered and made strange patterns on the wall, and the floorboards creaked eerily. At last, Clara took a deep breath and entered the room. Suddenly, there was a whirring noise and the owl on the grandfather clock flapped its wings. Clara gasped and fell to the floor, covering her face, while the clock struck twelve o'clock.

As Clara lay on the floor, two grey mice came running out of the shadows. They sniffed at her, then ran away. When the room was quiet again, Clara scrambled to her feet and ran to the Christmas tree. Just then, a large shadow—shaped like Dr. Drosselmeyer's cloak—fell across the room. Clara froze, not knowing what to do.

In another second, the shadow vanished and the most amazing thing happened: the Nutcracker, magically mended, came to life! He sprang to his feet and bowed to Clara, who curtsied politely back at him.

But there was no more time for introductions, for an army of great grey mice was pouring into the parlour. They were led by the Mouse King—a ferocious mouse with seven heads. The Nutcracker quickly called his own troops together, and Fritz's toy soldiers came marching into battle. Rifles flared and swords flashed, as the two armies met. Clara watched anxiously from the corner of the room. Many mice and toy soldiers were falling, wounded, to the floor. Before long, the Mouse King and the Nutcracker came face-to-face.

Clash! Clash! went the two leaders' swords. The Nutcracker fought bravely, but the Mouse King was too strong and too sly for him.

"Watch out!" cried Clara, as she watched the Mouse King run up to attack the Nutcracker from behind. Alarmed, she picked up one of her ballet slippers and threw it as hard as she could at the terrible, seven-headed mouse. The slipper hit the mouse in one of his faces, and the Mouse King was stunned. The Nutcracker quickly seized that moment to make his final charge.

The Mouse King fell dead to the ground, and the other mice soldiers fled. The Nutcracker and his soldiers were victorious!

Clara cheered. The Nutcracker stooped to pick up the ballet slipper and when he arose, he was no longer a wooden soldier. Instead, the Nutcracker had turned into a real, live Prince.

Still holding the slipper, the Prince walked over to Clara and dropped to one knee before her. "Thank you for saving my life," he said. The Prince then took the crown off the Mouse King and placed it on Clara's head. "I crown you Princess Clara," he said. "Please come and be my guest in the Kingdom of Sweets."

"Thank you!" said Clara.

With that, the two joined hands and began their journey.

III. The Land of Snow

With a royal sweep of his arm, the Prince cast the parlour walls away, and he and Clara stood in the midst of a beautiful winter wonderland. All about them were gentle snowbanks and fir trees. Falling snowflakes sparkled in the moonlight.

Little snowflake fairies circled about Clara to welcome her. When they melted away, more fairies appeared to dance around their visitor. Clara ran happily among them, while the air filled with lovely, light music—like fairy voices singing from the trees.

An elegant carriage made of half a walnut arrived to take Clara and the Prince to the Kingdom of Sweets. They climbed in and waved farewell to the Land of Snow. The silver-white fairies twirled and floated about them until the two were out of sight.

IV. The Kingdom of Sweets

Clara could hardly believe her eyes, as she and the Prince entered the enchanted kingdom. The palace walls were made of enormous, jelly-like blocks of Turkish delight, and the archways of marshmallows. The main entrance was adorned with carvings made from caramel and toffee, and enormous vases were filled with lemon custard and chocolate pudding.

The Sugar Plum Fairy, who ruled the Kingdom of Sweets, came fluttering down from her throne. She wore a pink, silk robe that was covered in delicate, crystallized sugar, as dainty as lace; on her head was a coronet of stars, which sparkled as she moved.

With a wave of the Sugar Plum Fairy's wand, a cook appeared behind a magical kitchen stove. Then more cooks appeared, stirring and whipping up all kinds of concoctions in large bowls. With another wave of her wand, several kitchen maids appeared and began to set a large table.

"How do you do, Princess Clara?" asked the Sugar Plum Fairy. "The Kingdom of Sweets is preparing a feast in your honour, because you saved our Prince's life. Please have a seat at the royal table."

Eyes wide with delight, Clara sat at the head of the table and was treated to the most delicious dishes in all the land. Later, the Sugar Plum Fairy led Clara to her throne to watch the entertainment the kingdom's Sweets had prepared.

Clara had never seen such dancing before. "I didn't know *sweets* could dance!" she exclaimed.

And yet there they were—funny, lively sweets—dancing! It was almost as if they were real people! First, the milk and dark chocolates did a fiery Spanish dance. Then three little marzipan shepherdesses stepped forward, skipping lightly while playing a song on their pipes. An agile pair of coffee-flavoured sweets, dressed in Arabian silks, did remarkable acrobatics.

But the most amazing sight of all was that of a giant lady bonbon, named Mother Ginger, who was dressed in a full, elegant hooped skirt. When she lifted her skirt, out tumbled dozens of smaller, brightly wrapped "sweets" that looked just like laughing, dancing children.

The highpoint of the evening was the Sugar Plum Fairy's own dance. It was a delight to watch the royal fairy twirl and spin and leap across the palace floor, for she was as light and graceful as spun sugar. The Fairy was then joined by her own prince, the Cavalier, who held her hand as she did beautiful little turns on the points of her toes. The Sugar Plum Fairy danced so lightly and easily, it seemed she might float away.

"She really *is* magic!" Clara thought to herself.

Clara wished she could stay in this land forever, but as dawn broke in the Kingdom of Sweets, she knew it was time to say goodbye. It was Christmas morning, and her family would be wondering where she was.

The Nutcracker Prince escorted Clara to the walnut carriage, which would take her home. The Prince kissed Clara lightly on the cheek and Clara smiled back at him.

As the carriage pulled away, the Sugar Plum Fairy, the cooks, kitchen maids, and all the Sweets waved goodbye to Princess Clara.

"Goodbye!" Clara called back. As she left, Clara was quite sure this wonderful adventure was the best Christmas gift she had ever received.

North Wind Picture Archives

FAVOURITE CHRISTMAS CAROLS

WE WISH YOU A MERRY CHRISTMAS

Text and Tune: Traditional English

We wish you a merry Christmas,
We wish you a merry Christmas,
We wish you a merry Christmas,
And a Happy New Year!

Good tidings we bring,
To you and your kin.
We wish you a merry Christmas,
And a Happy New Year!

We all want some figgy pudding,
We all want some figgy pudding,
We all want some figgy pudding,
So bring it right here!

GOOD KING WENCESLAS

J.M. Neale, translator from the Latin

Good King Wenceslas looked out
On the Feast of Stephen,
When the snow lay round about,
Deep and crisp, and even:
Brightly shone the moon that night,
Though the frost was cruel,
When a poor man came in sight,
Gath'ring winter fuel.

"Hither, page, and stand by me,
If thou know'st it; telling,
Yonder peasant, who is he?
Where and what his dwelling?"
"Sire, he lives a good league hence,
Underneath the mountain;
Right against the forest fence,
By Saint Agnes' fountain."

"Bring me flesh and bring me wine,
Bring me pinelogs hither;
Thou and I will see him dine,
When we bear them thither,"
Page and monarch forth they went,
Forth they went together;
Through the rude wind's wild lament,
And the bitter weather.

"Sire, the night is darker now,
And the wind blows stronger;
Fails my heart, I know not how,
I can go no longer."
"Mark my footsteps, my good page,
Tread thou in them boldly:
Thou shalt find the winter's rage,
Freeze thy blood less coldly."

In his master's steps he trod,
Where the snow lay dinted;
Heat was in the very sod
Which the saint had printed.
Therefore, Christian men, be sure,
Wealth or rank possessing,
"Ye who now will bless the poor,
Shall yourselves find blessing."

JOY TO THE WORLD

Text: Isaac Watts, 1719

Tune: Adapted from George F. Handel, 1742

Joy to the World!
The Lord is come;
Let earth receive her King;
Let every heart
Prepare Him room,
And heav'n and nature sing,
And heav'n and nature sing,
And heav'n and heav'n
And nature sing.

Joy to the world!
The Saviour reigns;
Let men their songs employ,
While fields and floods,
Rocks, hills, and plains
Repeat the sounding joy,
Repeat the sounding joy,
Repeat, repeat
The sounding joy.

THE TWELVE DAYS OF CHRISTMAS

Text and Tune: Traditional English

On the first day of Christmas my true
  love gave to me
A partridge in a pear tree.

On the second day of Christmas my true
  love gave to me
Two turtle doves, and a partridge in a
  pear tree.

On the third day of Christmas my true
  love gave to me
Three French hens, two turtle doves, and
  a partridge in a pear tree.

On the fourth day of Christmas my true
  love gave to me
Four calling birds, three French hens, two
  turtle doves, and a partridge in a pear
  tree.

On the fifth day of Christmas my true
  love gave to me
FIVE GOLDEN RINGS, four calling birds,
  three French hens, two turtle doves,
  and a partridge in a pear tree.

On the sixth . . . Six geese a-laying, (repeat
  previous ones)

On the seventh . . . Seven swans a-
  swimming, (repeat)

On the eighth . . . . Eight maids a-milking,
  (repeat)

On the ninth . . . . Nine ladies dancing,
  (repeat)

On the tenth . . . . Ten lords a-leaping,
  (repeat)

On the eleventh . . . . Eleven pipers piping,
  (repeat)

On the twelfth . . . . Twelve drummers
  drumming, (repeat)

HARK! THE HERALD ANGELS SING

Text: Charles Wesley, 1739   **Tune: Felix Mendelssohn, 1840**

Hark! the herald angels sing,
Glory to the newborn King;
Peace on earth, and mercy mild,
God and sinners reconciled!
Joyful all ye nations rise,
Join the triumph of the skies;
With th'angelic host proclaim,
Christ is born in Bethlehem.

REFRAIN:
Hark! the herald angels sing,
Glory to the newborn King.

Christ, by highest heaven adored,
Christ, the everlasting Lord,
Late in time behold him come,
Offspring of a Virgin's womb.
Veiled in flesh the Godhead see!
Hail, the incarnate Deity!
Pleased as Man with man to dwell,
Jesus, our Emmanuel.

(Refrain)

Hail, the heaven-born Prince of Peace!
Hail, the Sun of Righteousness!
Light and life to all he brings,
Risen with healing in his wings.
Mild he lays his glory by,
Born that man no more may die,
Born to raise the sons of earth,
Born to give them second birth.

(Refrain)

DECK THE HALLS

Text and Tune: Traditional Welsh

Deck the halls with boughs of holly,
Fa la la la la, la la la la;
'Tis the season to be jolly,
Fa la la la la, la la la la.
Don we now our gay apparel,
Fa la la, la la la, la la la.
Troll the ancient Yuletide carol
Fa la la la la, la la la la.

See the blazing Yule before us,
Fa la la la la, la la la la.
Strike the harp and join the chorus,
Fa la la la la, la la la la.
Follow me in merry measure,
Fa la la, la la la, la la la.
While I tell of Yuletide treasure,
Fa la la la la, la la la la.

AWAY IN A MANGER

Text: Anonymous   Tune: J.R. Murray, 1877

Away in a manger, no crib for a bed,
The little Lord Jesus laid down His sweet
    head.
The stars in the sky looked down where
    He lay,
The little Lord Jesus asleep on the hay.

The cattle are lowing, the poor Baby
    wakes,
But little Lord Jesus, no crying He makes.
I love thee, Lord Jesus, look down from
    the sky,
And stay by my cradle 'til morning is
    nigh.

WE THREE KINGS

Text and Tune: John H. Hopkins, 1857

We three kings of Orient are;
Bearing gifts, we traverse afar,
Field and fountain, moor and mountain,
Following yonder star.

REFRAIN:

O-oh! Star of wonder, star of night,
Star with royal beauty bright;
Westward leading, still proceeding,
Guide us to Thy perfect light.

Born a King on Bethlehem's plain,
Gold I bring to crown Him again,
King forever, ceasing never,
Over us all to reign.

(Refrain)

O LITTLE TOWN OF BETHLEHEM

Text: Philips Brooks   Tune: Lewis H. Redner

O little town of Bethlehem,
How still we see thee lie!
Above thy deep and dreamless sleep
The silent stars go by;
Yet in thy dark streets shineth
The everlasting Light;
The hopes and fears of all the years
Are met in thee tonight.

For Christ is born of Mary,
And gathered all above,
While mortals sleep, the angels keep
Their watch of wond'ring love.
O morning stars together
Proclaim the holy birth,
And praises sing to God the King,
And peace to men on earth!

O CHRISTMAS TREE!/ "O TANNENBAUM!"

(Original in German)   Text and Tune: Traditional German

O Christmas tree, O Christmas tree!
With faithful leaves unchanging;
Not only green in summer's heat,
But also winter's snow and sleet.
O Christmas tree, O Christmas tree!
With faithful leaves unchanging.

"O Tannenbaum, O Tannenbaum!
Wie treu sind deine Blätter!
Du grünst nicht nur in Sommerzeit,
Nein, auch im Winter, wenn es schneit.
O Tannenbaum, O Tannenbaum!
Wie treu sind deine Blätter!"

JINGLE BELLS

Text and Tune: James Pierpont

Dashing through the snow
In a one-horse open sleigh,
O'er the fields we go
Laughing all the way;
Bells on bobtails ring,
Making spirits bright;
What fun it is to laugh and sing
A sleighing song tonight—Oh!

Jingle bells, jingle bells,
Jingle all the way!
Oh, what fun it is to ride
In a one-horse open sleigh!
Jingle bells, jingle bells,
Jingle all the way!
Oh, what fun it is to ride
In a one-horse open sleigh!

BRING A TORCH, JEANNETTE, ISABELLA/
"UN FLAMBEAU, JEANNETTE, ISABELLE"

(Original in French)   Translation: E. Luthbert Nunn
Text: Traditional Provençal, 17th Century   Tune: 17th Century Provençal Carol

Bring a torch, Jeannette, Isabella,
Bring a torch to the cradle run!
It is Jesus, good folk of the village;
Christ is born and Mary's calling:
Ah! Ah! beautiful is the Mother,
Ah! Ah! beautiful is her Son!

"Un flambeau, Jeannette, Isabelle,
Un flambeau, courons au berceau!
C'est Jésus, bonnes gens du hameau,
Le Christ est né, Marie appelle,
Ah! Ah! que la mère est belle,
Ah! Ah! que l'Enfant est beau!"

Robert Grav

SILENT NIGHT, HOLY NIGHT/
"STILLE NACHT, HEILIGE NACHT"

(Original in German)

Text: Joseph Mohr, 1818   Tune: Franz Gruber, 1818   Translation: John F. Young, 1871

Silent night, Holy night;
All is calm, all is bright;
Round yon virgin Mother and Child.
Holy Infant so tender and mild,
Sleep in heavenly peace,
Sleep in heavenly peace.

Silent night, Holy night;
Shepherds quake at the sight;
Glories stream from heaven afar,
Heavenly hosts sing alleluia.
Christ, the Saviour is born!
Christ, the Saviour is born!

"Stille Nacht, Heilige Nacht;
All' schläft, einsam wacht,
Nur das traute hoch heilige Paar.
Holder Knabe im lockigen Haar,
Schlaf in himmlischer Ruh,
Schlaf in himmlischer Ruh."

O COME, ALL YE FAITHFUL/
"ADESTE FIDELIS"

Text and Tune: John Wade, c. 1740   (Original in Latin)   Translation: Frederick Oakley, 1841

O come, all ye faithful,
Joyful and triumphant,
O come, ye; O come ye,
To Bethlehem.
Come and behold Him,
Born the King of Angels;

REFRAIN:

O come, let us adore Him,
O come, let us adore Him,
O come, let us adore Him,
Christ, the Lord!

Sing, choirs of angels,
Sing in exultation,
Sing all ye citizens of heav'n above!
Glory to God, all glory in the highest!

(Refrain) (Cont'd., in Latin)

"Adeste fideles, Laeti triumphantes,
Venite, venite in Bethlehem!
Natum videte,
Regem angelorum;
Venite adoremus,
Venite adoremus,
Venite adoremus,
Dominum!"

Robert Gray

Robert Gray

METRIC CONVERSIONS

Use the table of measures below to convert from metric to U.S. measures and vice versa. All conversions are approximate.

DRY WEIGHT MEASURES

25 grams	1 ounce	1 tablespoon
55 grams	2 ounces	¼ cup
85 grams	3 ounces	⅓ cup
110 grams	4 ounces	½ cup
170 grams	6 ounces	¾ cup
225 grams	8 ounces	1 cup
280 grams	10 ounces	1¼ cup
340 grams	12 ounces	1½ cup
450 grams	1 pound	2 cups
560 grams	1 pound, 4 ounces	2½ cups
675 grams	1½ pounds	3 cups

LIQUID MEASURES

30 millilitres	1 fluid ounce	⅛ cup
55 millilitres	2 fluid ounces	¼ cup
85 millilitres	3 fluid ounces	¾ cup
250 millilitres	11 fluid ounces	1 cup
340 millilitres	12 fluid ounces	1½ cups
450 millilitres	16 fluid ounces	2 cups
785 millilitres	28 fluid ounces	2¼ cups
1 litre	34 fluid ounces	1¾ pints

OVEN TEMPERATURES

300°F	150°C	Gas Mark 2
325°F	160°C	Gas Mark 3
350°F	180°C	Gas Mark 4
375°F	190°C	Gas Mark 5
400°F	200°C	Gas Mark 6

LENGTH

½ centimetre	⅛ inch
1 centimetre	¼ inch
2½ centimetres	1 inch
5 centimetres	2 inches
10 centimetres	4 inches
20 centimetres	8 inches

INDEX

Recipe titles are in italics; page numbers in italics refer to captions and illustrations.